JUMBLE FARM

A Pasture of Puzzles!

David L. Hoyt
and
Jeff Knurek

TRIUMPH
BOOKS

Jumble® is a registered trademark
of Tribune Media Services, Inc.
Copyright © 2023 by Tribune Media Services, Inc.
All rights reserved.
This book is available in quantity at special discounts
for your group or organization.

For further information, con tact:
Triumph Books LLC
814 North Franklin Street
Chicago, Illinois 60610
Phone: (312) 337-0747
www.triumphbooks.com

Printed in U.S.A.

ISBN: 978-1-63727-460-6

Design by Sue Knopf

CONTENTS

JUMBLE®

FARM

CLASSIC PUZZLE

JUMBLE®

Unscramble these four Jumbles, one letter to each square, to form four ordinary words.

IRICE

SMRTU

TREFER

SLOJET

I can't believe you've never cooked before!

You like my appetizer!

SHE KNEW SHE WANTED TO BE A CHEF AFTER HER ---

Now arrange the circled letters to form the surprise answer, as suggested by the above cartoon.

Print answer here

2

JUMBLE®

Unscramble these four Jumbles, one letter
to each square, to form four ordinary words.

VOBEA

RUYHR

ZANYSZ

THEARF

Hey! I hope you had a lot of rides tonight. You owe me half the rent and internet.

It was raining! We're all good. I bought us a pizza.

DRIVING PEOPLE FROM PLACE TO PLACE ALLOWED HIM TO BRING HOME HIS ---

Now arrange the circled letters
to form the surprise answer, as
suggested by the above cartoon.

Print answer " ◯◯◯◯ " ◯◯◯◯◯
here

3

JUMBLE®

Unscramble these four Jumbles, one letter to each square, to form four ordinary words.

PENIT

TIYWT

LOLWEM

TYEALL

We need to put out a press release soon.

I think we have it narrowed down.

WHO IS GOING TO BE THE MAGAZINE'S NEXT "PERSON OF THE YEAR"?

Now arrange the circled letters to form the surprise answer, as suggested by the above cartoon.

Print answer here

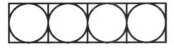 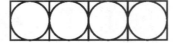 

JUMBLE®

Unscramble these four Jumbles, one letter to each square, to form four ordinary words.

VUGAA

MHOUR

KRYAEB

GORDAN

What do you have against him?

He stole a barge job from me once.

THE TUGBOAT OPERATOR WAS NOT VERY FORGIVING AND KNOWN TO ---

Now arrange the circled letters to form the surprise answer, as suggested by the above cartoon.

Print answer here

JUMBLE®

Unscramble these four Jumbles, one letter to each square, to form four ordinary words.

LAVEH

BOTIR

SIBYUL

CNEHRT

The show is about humankind. Warp speed and phasers are just tools to tell the story.

It's brilliant.

Maybe we'll get to kiss.

I get to do a lot of kissing.

WITH "STAR TREK," GENE RODDENBERRY SHOWED US A POSSIBLE FUTURE. HE WAS A ---

Now arrange the circled letters to form the surprise answer, as suggested by the above cartoon.

Print answer here

" ◯◯◯◯◯◯◯◯◯◯◯◯◯◯ "

JUMBLE®

Unscramble these four Jumbles, one letter
to each square, to form four ordinary words.

LYALR

SRNOW

VCNASA

TVICEA

It sure
is sunny!

It's so
peaceful.

We have
the whole
beach to
ourselves.

THE RAIN HAD STOPPED. THEY
COULD GO TO THE BEACH
NOW THAT THE ---

Now arrange the circled letters
to form the surprise answer, as
suggested by the above cartoon.

Print
answer
here

JUMBLE®

Unscramble these four Jumbles, one letter to each square, to form four ordinary words.

PENIT

PRIVE

GFSNUU

DEMEIP

TO SEE PROOF THAT THE CAR WASN'T WELL-CARED-FOR, HE LOOKED AT THE ---

Now arrange the circled letters to form the surprise answer, as suggested by the above cartoon.

Print answer here " ◯◯◯ - ◯◯◯◯◯ "

JUMBLE®

Unscramble these four Jumbles, one letter
to each square, to form four ordinary words.

NKUYF

BAMMO

PRANDO

NNUEKS

We found them.

It looks like fun.

THE BABOONS RODE
THE CAROUSEL AT THE
AMUSEMENT PARK BECAUSE
THEY WANTED TO ---

Now arrange the circled letters
to form the surprise answer, as
suggested by the above cartoon.

Print answer here

JUMBLE®

Unscramble these four Jumbles, one letter to each square, to form four ordinary words.

VRLAA

GTURN

BARNET

SCOHOM

THE CROW WHO CONSIDERED HERSELF TO BE IN CHARGE OF ROOSTING WAS THE ---

Now arrange the circled letters to form the surprise answer, as suggested by the above cartoon.

Print answer here

JUMBLE®

Unscramble these four Jumbles, one letter to each square, to form four ordinary words.

VACHO

GREME

TTREEH

MOSLAN

Whoa! Look at him stretch!

The guys who wrote this, Lee and Kirby, are brilliant!

I love the Invisible Girl!

WHEN "THE FANTASTIC FOUR" DEBUTED, READERS BOUGHT THE COMIC BOOKS TO ---

Now arrange the circled letters to form the surprise answer, as suggested by the above cartoon.

 Print answer here

JUMBLE®

Unscramble these four Jumbles, one letter to each square, to form four ordinary words.

NIRKD

DOORE

VOILJA

MMIDUE

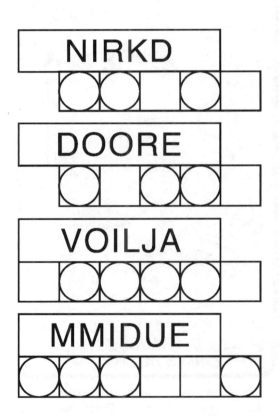

SHE WAS BECOMING ANGRIER, BUT, AFTER THINKING ABOUT IT, IT WAS ---

Now arrange the circled letters to form the surprise answer, as suggested by the above cartoon.

Print answer here

"   "

12

JUMBLE

Unscramble these four Jumbles, one letter
to each square, to form four ordinary words.

LIRGL

SLOAS

LIMWED

CABONE

This
makes
me so
nervous.

I can't
watch!

I can't
believe
this.

HE SCALED YOSEMITE'S
"EL CAPITAN" WITHOUT
A ROPE, WHICH HAD
ONLOOKERS ---

Now arrange the circled letters
to form the surprise answer, as
suggested by the above cartoon.

**Print
answer
here**

THE

13

JUMBLE®

Unscramble these four Jumbles, one letter
to each square, to form four ordinary words.

DAIVO

DEEGW

UCPPKI

NVEEEL

We're just finessing it in place.

You're too loud! I'm trying to talk on the phone!

THE INSTALLATION OF THE NEW
SINK WAS VERY NOISY. SHE
WANTED THE PLUMBERS TO ---

Now arrange the circled letters
to form the surprise answer, as
suggested by the above cartoon.

Print answer here

14

JUMBLE®

Unscramble these four Jumbles, one letter
to each square, to form four ordinary words.

GADAE

CASHO

RROEPP

LAEBBB

Isn't this paradise?

It's made for us.

IF WILD PIGS COULD LIVE
ANYWHERE IN THE WORLD,
THEY MIGHT CHOOSE ---

Now arrange the circled letters
to form the surprise answer, as
suggested by the above cartoon.

**Print
answer
here** " ◯◯◯◯-◯   ◯◯◯◯-◯ "

JUMBLE®

Unscramble these four Jumbles, one letter to each square, to form four ordinary words.

AVEWE

NRITP

CENDRH

ROCAGU

I can't wait until this is open again.

It's always being fixed.

CLOSED

Do Not Cross   Construction

THEY USED THE SUBWAY TO GO TO WORK EVERY DAY EXCEPT WHEN IT WAS ---

Now arrange the circled letters to form the surprise answer, as suggested by the above cartoon.

Print answer here

16

JUMBLE®

Unscramble these four Jumbles, one letter
to each square, to form four ordinary words.

PERTC

MLOBO

BUSTIM

FLUREF

You wanna
go head-to-
head, or are
you too
scared?

Who are they
trying to
impress?

Let's do
this!

WHEN THE RAM ASKED HIS
ADVERSARY IF HE WANTED
TO FIGHT, HE REPLIED ---

Now arrange the circled letters
to form the surprise answer, as
suggested by the above cartoon.

Print
answer
here " ⬡⬡⬡⬡ " ⬡⬡ ⬡⬡⬡⬡⬡⬡

JUMBLE®

Unscramble these four Jumbles, one letter
to each square, to form four ordinary words.

FRWEA

NUYNS

FTRADY

DOUSIT

We have to get this right. Which vaccine should we recommend?

I can't think straight.

TRYING TO IDENTIFY AND DEAL WITH ALL THE DIFFERENT TYPES OF FLU WAS A ---

Now arrange the circled letters
to form the surprise answer, as
suggested by the above cartoon.

Print answer here

THE

JUMBLE®

Unscramble these four Jumbles, one letter to each square, to form four ordinary words.

MELPI

ORDUP

TURFHO

CIYPER

Will you still love me after I lose my bounce?

You will always be my snuggle bunny.

THE RABBITS HAD BEEN MARRIED FOR YEARS AND WERE A ---

Now arrange the circled letters to form the surprise answer, as suggested by the above cartoon.

Print answer here

JUMBLE®

Unscramble these four Jumbles, one letter to each square, to form four ordinary words.

TAMDI

WPORE

CISYKT

GHRBTI

I just need everyone to look busy.

What's my motivation?

THE MOVIE SCENE BEING FILMED IN THE MACHINE SHOP FEATURED ---

Now arrange the circled letters to form the surprise answer, as suggested by the above cartoon.

Print answer here

20

JUMBLE®

Unscramble these four Jumbles, one letter to each square, to form four ordinary words.

MILTI

CLUKA

MRIEBL

TEYNIT

Our friends said you're the best!

Word of mouth is my favorite advertisement.

THE LAWYER PICKED UP NEW BUSINESS BECAUSE HER HAPPY CUSTOMERS WERE ---

Now arrange the circled letters to form the surprise answer, as suggested by the above cartoon.

Print answer here

" ◯◯◯◯◯◯ - ◯◯◯◯ "

JUMBLE®

Unscramble these four Jumbles, one letter to each square, to form four ordinary words.

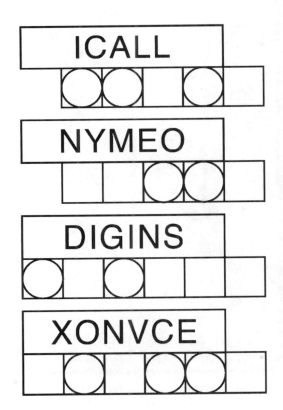

ICALL

NYMEO

DIGINS

XONVCE

I wrote the monster as a sympathetic character representing the weakest among us.

It's amazing. How original.

MARY SHELLEY'S SUCCESS AS AN AUTHOR WAS A RESULT OF HER HAVING ---

Now arrange the circled letters to form the surprise answer, as suggested by the above cartoon.

Print answer here

JUMBLE®

Unscramble these four Jumbles, one letter to each square, to form four ordinary words.

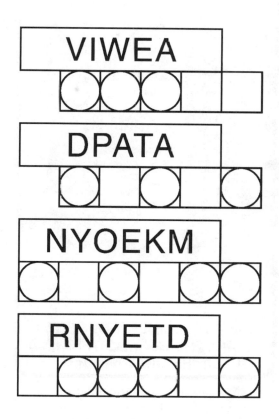

VIWEA

DPATA

NYOEKM

RNYETD

My bags are packed. I can be there when you'd like.

I can give you a ride to the airport.

THE FASHION MODEL WAS VERY FLEXIBLE AND WILLING TO WORK ---

Now arrange the circled letters to form the surprise answer, as suggested by the above cartoon.

Print answer here

 - "  "

JUMBLE®

Unscramble these four Jumbles, one letter to each square, to form four ordinary words.

TUYTN

NOGGI

CLNIEH

SANEFT

There! That's the place.

We almost went right past it.

THE ANGLER KNEW HE'D FOUND THE PERFECT FISHING SPOT THE MOMENT HE ---

Now arrange the circled letters to form the surprise answer, as suggested by the above cartoon.

Print answer here

JUMBLE

Unscramble these four Jumbles, one letter to each square, to form four ordinary words.

THOYL

RATAP

WORDSY

SWYILE

There is no way you can do that!

Just watch me!

Dude! I can barely choke this down.

HIS CLAIM THAT HE COULD EAT A HOT DOG IN JUST TWO BITES WAS ---

Now arrange the circled letters to form the surprise answer, as suggested by the above cartoon.

Print answer here

JUMBLE®

Unscramble these four Jumbles, one letter to each square, to form four ordinary words.

AMULQ

RJEKO

DZCOIA

PRIZEP

WHEN PEOPLE FIRST SAW COUNT BASIE PERFORM, THEY WERE ---

Now arrange the circled letters to form the surprise answer, as suggested by the above cartoon.

Print answer here

JUMBLE® FARM

DAILY
PUZZLE

JUMBLE®

Unscramble these four Jumbles, one letter to each square, to form four ordinary words.

EGRIT

NRKAC

PAHNEP

MIYOHL

Barb said this is a knockoff.

Isn't your wife worth more, Hal?

Um. Uh. It's just a temporary one until they get the real one in.

HIS WIFE FOUND OUT THAT HER NEW RING WAS A CHEAP IMITATION, AND NOW HE'D ---

Now arrange the circled letters to form the surprise answer, as suggested by the above cartoon.

Print answer here

JUMBLE®

Unscramble these four Jumbles, one letter to each square, to form four ordinary words.

REAVB

CORPH

LERRAY

RRROIM

I don't know. They're both the same price. I could see myself in both.

Either would be fine on you.

IT WAS HARD TO CHOOSE WHICH NEW SOCKS TO BUY BECAUSE THEY WERE SO ---

Now arrange the circled letters to form the surprise answer, as suggested by the above cartoon.

Print answer here

" ☐☐☐ - ☐☐☐☐ - ☐☐☐☐ "

JUMBLE®

Unscramble these four Jumbles, one letter to each square, to form four ordinary words.

SUFHL

ENOYH

DARTIE

FESYAL

That didn't last long.

You get what you pay for.

THE BOOKCASE WASN'T MADE VERY WELL AND HAD A ---

Now arrange the circled letters to form the surprise answer, as suggested by the above cartoon.

Print answer here

JUMBLE®

Unscramble these four Jumbles, one letter to each square, to form four ordinary words.

CANKK

TIHDC

PLUCEO

BOLTEG

You all are so sweet.

THE CAT GAVE BIRTH TO A HUGE LITTER, AND SHE LOVED THE WHOLE ---

Now arrange the circled letters to form the surprise answer, as suggested by the above cartoon.

Print answer here

" ◯◯◯◯◯◯ " ◯◯◯◯◯◯◯◯◯

JUMBLE®

Unscramble these four Jumbles, one letter to each square, to form four ordinary words.

BOYHB

TUHRT

EEEDRM

AUTMTE

Again? What are you doing differently?

I'm being more patient. And bluffing less.

HE STARTED WINNING MORE POKER TOURNAMENTS AFTER BECOMING A ---

Now arrange the circled letters to form the surprise answer, as suggested by the above cartoon.

Print answer here

JUMBLE®

Unscramble these four Jumbles, one letter
to each square, to form four ordinary words.

OCTLU

DDAYD

FETFEC

SECEEH

You're ready to take over our business.

I could never replace you, Dad.

HER FATHER HANDED
THE BUSINESS OVER
TO HER, AND SHE ---

Now arrange the circled letters
to form the surprise answer, as
suggested by the above cartoon.

Print answer here

JUMBLE®

Unscramble these four Jumbles, one letter to each square, to form four ordinary words.

ERMIP

JYEON

TONKYT

DAYTIN

You look nothing like the original Klingons. Kirk would laugh at you.

That's because the makeup got better in later series.

HE LOVED KIRK, SPOCK, THE ENTERPRISE, ETC. AND HAD A ---

Now arrange the circled letters to form the surprise answer, as suggested by the above cartoon.

Print answer here

 "  "

JUMBLE®

Unscramble these four Jumbles, one letter
to each square, to form four ordinary words.

RUBYL

DYASI

TLOCEH

ULYBBB

We'll get this
sanitized and
reschedule
for next
week.

I'll tell
the crew.

AFTER FINDING
CONTAMINANTS IN THE NEW
SPACE CAPSULE, THE TEST
FLIGHT HAD TO BE ---

Now arrange the circled letters
to form the surprise answer, as
suggested by the above cartoon.

Print answer here

JUMBLE®

Unscramble these four Jumbles, one letter to each square, to form four ordinary words.

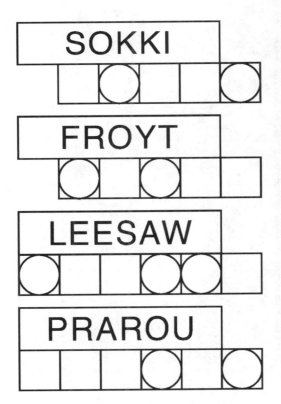

SOKKI

FROYT

LEESAW

PRAROU

My lighter is out.

Here you go.

RED WHITE and BOOM!!!

WHEN IT COMES TO LIGHTING THE FUSES FOR ALL THE 4TH OF JULY PYROTECHNIC DISPLAYS, ---

Now arrange the circled letters to form the surprise answer, as suggested by the above cartoon.

Print answer here

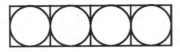 

JUMBLE®

Unscramble these four Jumbles, one letter to each square, to form four ordinary words.

FEYTH

DEYSE

TCLIGH

CLORAL

What?!

Look, Mommy! I'm a big girl!

WHEN THE LITTLE GIRL LEARNED TO USE SCISSORS, THE RESULT WAS ---

Now arrange the circled letters to form the surprise answer, as suggested by the above cartoon.

Print answer here " ☐☐☐☐☐ " ☐☐☐☐☐☐☐☐

JUMBLE®

Unscramble these four Jumbles, one letter
to each square, to form four ordinary words.

GUHRO

GOCIL

DWWION

DTIFET

I need you to go
to every faucet
and check for
pressure.

No problem.
I'll get right
on it.

THE NEW PLUMBER WAS VERY
EASY TO GET ALONG WITH
AND HAPPY TO ---

Now arrange the circled letters
to form the surprise answer, as
suggested by the above cartoon.

Print answer here

☐☐ ☐☐☐☐ **THE** ☐☐☐☐

38

JUMBLE®

Unscramble these four Jumbles, one letter to each square, to form four ordinary words.

RIWTL

SEMSY

PSOOEP

NEIYNT

Nice swing!

That's a home run!

Candy!

THE BIRTHDAY BOY SWUNG THE BAT AND CAUGHT THE PIÑATA RIGHT IN THE ---

Now arrange the circled letters to form the surprise answer, as suggested by the above cartoon.

Print answer here

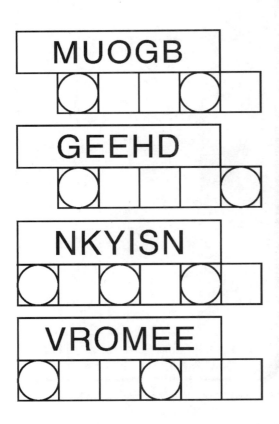

JUMBLE®

Unscramble these four Jumbles, one letter to each square, to form four ordinary words.

MUOGB

GEEHD

NKYISN

VROMEE

A pleasure to meet you.

Your horse will love it here!

THEY BOUGHT A HOME WHERE HORSES WERE ALLOWED AND LOVED THEIR ---

Now arrange the circled letters to form the surprise answer, as suggested by the above cartoon.

Print answer here

" ◯◯◯◯◯ - ◯◯◯◯ "

JUMBLE®

Unscramble these four Jumbles, one letter
to each square, to form four ordinary words.

SUYMT

VOHES

EBOWLB

TDERON

WHEN CONGRESS
CREATED THE U.S. MINT IN
1792, THEY GOT THEIR ---

Now arrange the circled letters
to form the surprise answer, as
suggested by the above cartoon.

**Print
answer
here**

JUMBLE®

Unscramble these four Jumbles, one letter
to each square, to form four ordinary words.

GTURO

NRTIP

TCOEKD

TTUFIO

Looks like
you got two
more stars
for us!

They're
the real
deal!

THE MAJOR LEAGUE SOCCER
SCOUT'S EFFECT ON THE
TEAM WAS ---

Now arrange the circled letters
to form the surprise answer, as
suggested by the above cartoon.

Print answer
here   "◯◯◯ - ◯◯◯◯◯"

JUMBLE®

Unscramble these four Jumbles, one letter
to each square, to form four ordinary words.

OHRNO

INYUT

DRIMEA

CUCEAR

Next!

Here.
Good luck!
Don't give
him any
combos.

Thanks
for the
info.

IT WAS HIS TURN AT THE
POOL TABLE NOW THAT THE
PREVIOUS PLAYER HAD ---

Now arrange the circled letters
to form the surprise answer, as
suggested by the above cartoon.

*Print
answer
here*

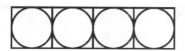

43

JUMBLE®

Unscramble these four Jumbles, one letter to each square, to form four ordinary words.

KARPN

GUAVE

DSMWIO

NLAHED

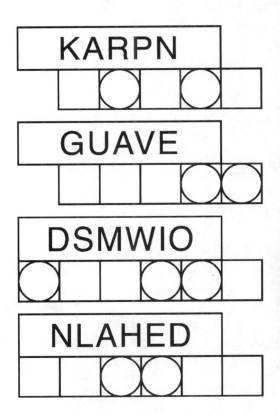

THE SUBMARINE IN THE SEA BETWEEN AUSTRALIA AND NEW ZEALAND WAS ---

Now arrange the circled letters to form the surprise answer, as suggested by the above cartoon.

Print answer here

JUMBLE®

Unscramble these four Jumbles, one letter to each square, to form four ordinary words.

SOYBS

ENBAG

SCRITT

KUEPEP

Can I open your schedule up again?

Yes. My vacation's over.

WHEN THE CHIROPRACTOR RETURNED FROM VACATION, IT WAS ---

Now arrange the circled letters to form the surprise answer, as suggested by the above cartoon.

Print answer here

JUMBLE®

Unscramble these four Jumbles, one letter to each square, to form four ordinary words.

IDTGI

MUNHA

DPAENX

DILEMD

This was just dropped off. Can you get it sewn today?

Sure. I don't think I'm going anywhere.

ALL THE NEW DRESS ORDERS HAD THE SEAMSTRESS FEELING ---

Now arrange the circled letters to form the surprise answer, as suggested by the above cartoon.

Print answer here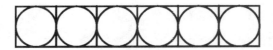

JUMBLE®

Unscramble these four Jumbles, one letter
to each square, to form four ordinary words.

VROHE

NHIYS

PIAMHS

DOYBIL

Looking good, troops.
Make us proud.

THE RESPECTFUL TROOPS
CALLED THE GENERAL ---

Now arrange the circled letters
to form the surprise answer, as
suggested by the above cartoon.

Print
answer
here

JUMBLE®

Unscramble these four Jumbles, one letter to each square, to form four ordinary words.

RMUYK

HAALO

TAWEYS

GRREUB

Are we ready to start delivering?

That's what we trained for.

I love this job!

THE OBSTETRICIANS STARTED THEIR BUSINESS TOGETHER, AND NOW THEY'RE PART OF THE ---

Now arrange the circled letters to form the surprise answer, as suggested by the above cartoon.

Print answer here

JUMBLE®

Unscramble these four Jumbles, one letter to each square, to form four ordinary words.

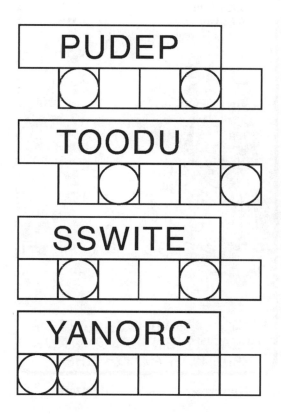

PUDEP

TOODU

SSWITE

YANORC

Have you found what you're looking for?

I think so, but I'm still perplexed about a few things.

ALEXANDER FLEMING DISCOVERED ANTIBIOTICS IN 1928 THANKS IN PART TO HIM BEING ---

Now arrange the circled letters to form the surprise answer, as suggested by the above cartoon.

Print answer here " ⬡⬡⬡⬡⬡ - ⬡⬡⬡⬡⬡ "

JUMBLE®

Unscramble these four Jumbles, one letter to each square, to form four ordinary words.

DHGEE

ALIYD

SAQYUE

KAMBER

We want the castles, the cars and all the caskets.

Whoa! You're leaving him with nothing.

It was just a nibble.

DRACULA'S WIFE CAUGHT HIM CHEATING ON HER, AND NOW SHE WAS GOING TO ---

Now arrange the circled letters to form the surprise answer, as suggested by the above cartoon.

Print answer here

JUMBLE®

Unscramble these four Jumbles, one letter
to each square, to form four ordinary words.

LBYUK

FINFS

AHREDR

ADLPED

THE WASHED-UP COFFEE
GROWER WAS A ---

Now arrange the circled letters
to form the surprise answer, as
suggested by the above cartoon.

Print answer here "   "

JUMBLE®

Unscramble these four Jumbles, one letter
to each square, to form four ordinary words.

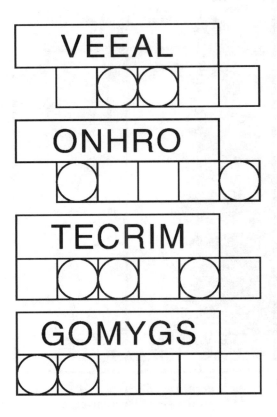

VEEAL

ONHRO

TECRIM

GOMYGS

I have a few
occasions
coming up
when I need
to wear
this.

I'm going to need it
for my daughter's
wedding next month.

WHEN THE BROTHERS
TOOK TURNS WEARING
THEIR GRANDFATHER'S
WATCH, IT WAS A ---

Now arrange the circled letters
to form the surprise answer, as
suggested by the above cartoon.

**Print answer
here**

JUMBLE®

Unscramble these four Jumbles, one letter
to each square, to form four ordinary words.

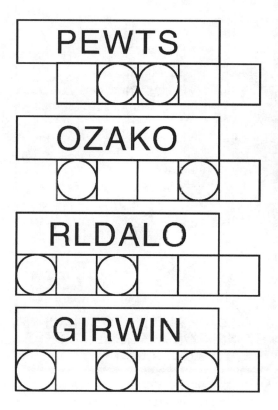

PEWTS

OZAKO

RLDALO

GIRWIN

So, you are saying that this is what the Americas look like?

It was created from everything we have learned.

AFTER THE WESTERN
HEMISPHERE WAS MAPPED
IN THE EARLY 1500S,
IT WAS THE ---

Now arrange the circled letters
to form the surprise answer, as
suggested by the above cartoon.

Print answer here " ◯◯◯◯ " ◯◯◯◯◯

JUMBLE®

Unscramble these four Jumbles, one letter to each square, to form four ordinary words.

CVOTE

LDAAS

PAOTUI

ARFELT

Dispersing all those satellites will take some time.

Wow! This is a record-breaking number of satellites for a single rocket!

THE 104 SATELLITES LAUNCHED BY INDIA ON A SINGLE ROCKET WOULD GET ---

Now arrange the circled letters to form the surprise answer, as suggested by the above cartoon.

Print answer here

JUMBLE®

Unscramble these four Jumbles, one letter to each square, to form four ordinary words.

CTAFE

NRLEI

DOLDOE

DDDEEW

I found it online! It's filled with goose feathers.

Where did you get the new pillow?

THE COMPUTER PROGRAMMER LOVED HIS NEW PILLOW BECAUSE IT WAS ---

Now arrange the circled letters to form the surprise answer, as suggested by the above cartoon.

Print answer here ◯◯◯◯ - ◯◯◯◯◯◯◯

JUMBLE®

Unscramble these four Jumbles, one letter to each square, to form four ordinary words.

MLBIP

THHIC

DOLCED

NRIYWE

They're all located for the best results.

Thank you for all your effort.

Yes. Thank you.

THEY HIRED AN EXPERT OIL DRILLER WHO ---

Now arrange the circled letters to form the surprise answer, as suggested by the above cartoon.

Print answer here

56

JUMBLE®

Unscramble these four Jumbles, one letter to each square, to form four ordinary words.

NBCHE

LIMKY

TAKEAR

TWULAN

How many of these have you done?

I've lost track. I could do these in my sleep.

THE CARDIOLOGIST HAD PERFORMED THE PROCEDURE SO MANY TIMES, SHE ---

Now arrange the circled letters to form the surprise answer, as suggested by the above cartoon.

Print answer here

JUMBLE®

Unscramble these four Jumbles, one letter
to each square, to form four ordinary words.

RYRAA

SOYUL

TOLIVE

NNFAIT

The only
conclusion can be
that the planets
circle the sun.

Be careful who
you share that
theory with.

WHEN COPERNICUS THEORIZED
THAT THE EARTH WENT
AROUND THE SUN, IT WAS ---

Now arrange the circled letters
to form the surprise answer, as
suggested by the above cartoon.

**Print
answer
here**

JUMBLE®

Unscramble these four Jumbles, one letter
to each square, to form four ordinary words.

AATRO

DLAGN

TERYPT

DIORNO

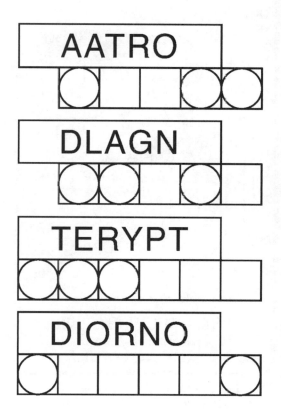

I thought Kong was a big sweetie.

This movie is going to be a huge hit!

TICKETS

SHOWING

KING KONG

KING KONG'S SUCCESS
IN THEATERS WAS DUE TO
ITS MAIN CHARACTER, ---

Now arrange the circled letters
to form the surprise answer, as
suggested by the above cartoon.

 Print answer here

JUMBLE®

Unscramble these four Jumbles, one letter
to each square, to form four ordinary words.

HIYTC

NGIES

THIUSA

NGOYPS

Oh,
no.

SYSTEM
FAILURE

WHEN THEIR FUSION
EXPERIMENT FAILED, THE
RESEARCHERS WERE ---

Now arrange the circled letters
to form the surprise answer, as
suggested by the above cartoon.

**Print
answer
here**   " ⬡⬡⬡⬡ - ⬡⬡⬡⬡⬡⬡⬡ "

JUMBLE®

Unscramble these four Jumbles, one letter to each square, to form four ordinary words.

ALGEE

VIOEM

SEKONP

CILATI

No one compares to me at work.

You and me both. We're great.

THE NARCISSISTS WHO GOT ALONG SO WELL WERE AT THE - - -

Now arrange the circled letters to form the surprise answer, as suggested by the above cartoon.

Print answer here

"□"

JUMBLE®

Unscramble these four Jumbles, one letter to each square, to form four ordinary words.

SYCIP

UNDOW

GLEYCR

PHIBSO

I really need the practice.

Remember, we'll be back tomorrow to play too.

THE GOLFERS WANTED TO USE THE DRIVING RANGE, SO THEY DECIDED TO ---

Now arrange the circled letters to form the surprise answer, as suggested by the above cartoon.

Print answer here ◯◯◯◯◯ ◯◯ THE ◯◯◯◯◯◯

JUMBLE®

Unscramble these four Jumbles, one letter to each square, to form four ordinary words.

RIFTL

SUDEO

FRETOF

NSAATZ

You should give up painting. You're a master at this.

AFTER HIS THIRD BULL'S-EYE IN A ROW, IT WAS CLEAR THAT VINCENT VAN GOGH WAS A ---

Now arrange the circled letters to form the surprise answer, as suggested by the above cartoon.

Print answer here " ◯◯◯◯ - ◯◯◯ "

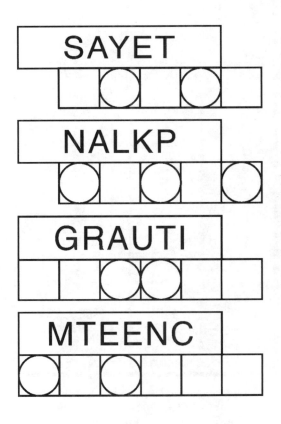

JUMBLE®

Unscramble these four Jumbles, one letter
to each square, to form four ordinary words.

SAYET

NALKP

GRAUTI

MTEENC

Wait until you hear this. I put all my favorite songs of his on it.

I hope you have his duo with Bowie on it.

SHE LOVED ALL OF
JAGGER'S MUSIC,
SO SHE MADE A ---

Now arrange the circled letters
to form the surprise answer, as
suggested by the above cartoon.

Print
answer
here

" ◯◯◯◯ ' ◯ " ◯◯◯◯

JUMBLE®

Unscramble these four Jumbles, one letter
to each square, to form four ordinary words.

DULEE

NUHBC

SSMCOO

LAZETO

- Whoa! This hasn't been aired out in a while.

Let's open the windows and get the moldy smell out of here.

WHEN SOMETHING STARTS
TO SMELL MOLDY AND
STALE, IT ---

Now arrange the circled letters
to form the surprise answer, as
suggested by the above cartoon.

Print answer here

JUMBLE®

Unscramble these four Jumbles, one letter
to each square, to form four ordinary words.

COLFA

CRIHP

NEOUFD

LRIHLS

Thanks!
That hit
the spot!

That car doesn't
look 65 years old!

I was
starving!

THEY GOT HUNGRY WHILE
WAXING THEIR CAR, SO
THEY STOPPED TO ---

Now arrange the circled letters
to form the surprise answer, as
suggested by the above cartoon.

**Print
answer
here**

JUMBLE®

Unscramble these four Jumbles, one letter
to each square, to form four ordinary words.

LAFEB

FEITH

TAATNI

DOMUPI

PEOPLE AT THE LABOR DAY
COOKOUT STRUGGLED WHEN
THE MOSQUITOES ---

Now arrange the circled letters
to form the surprise answer, as
suggested by the above cartoon.

Print
answer
here

JUMBLE®

Unscramble these four Jumbles, one letter to each square, to form four ordinary words.

SLUPH

WDROC

LUYFAT

OIMNEC

Everyone's looking good today.

No one wants the intern to be the best-dressed employee.

ONCE ONE OFFICE WORKER STARTED WEARING BUSINESS ATTIRE TO WORK, OTHERS ---

Now arrange the circled letters to form the surprise answer, as suggested by the above cartoon.

Print answer here

JUMBLE®

Unscramble these four Jumbles, one letter to each square, to form four ordinary words.

VINGE

CHOTN

MONIRF

GGLGEA

Weren't you going to write a big word book?

It's a book with definitions of words. I'm still planning on it.

NOAH WEBSTER HADN'T STARTED WORK ON HIS DICTIONARY YET, BUT HE WAS ---

Now arrange the circled letters to form the surprise answer, as suggested by the above cartoon.

Print answer here

JUMBLE®

Unscramble these four Jumbles, one letter to each square, to form four ordinary words.

LATVE

NHUMC

VREALG

OGLONB

Here are your tickets. You're on the next flight. Are you ready to go?

I'm ready to go!

SHE WAS TRANSFERRING TO THEIR LONDON OFFICE, SO THEY WANTED HER TO ---

Now arrange the circled letters to form the surprise answer, as suggested by the above cartoon.

Print answer here

JUMBLE®

Unscramble these four Jumbles, one letter to each square, to form four ordinary words.

VONLE

HEWIL

ROTEXT

IDIACC

I guess we can't stay here.

There are plenty of other branches for our home.

THE BRANCH DIDN'T WORK FOR BUILDING THEIR NEST, BUT THE BIRDS WEREN'T GOING TO ---

Now arrange the circled letters to form the surprise answer, as suggested by the above cartoon.

Print answer here

JUMBLE®

Unscramble these four Jumbles, one letter to each square, to form four ordinary words.

NUYFN

PIRGE

CIFLEK

SECASC

I could make it to the other side easily.

No way! It's too far. You're crazy.

NO ONE COULD SWIM ACROSS THE PARIS RIVER UNDERWATER. THAT WOULD BE ---

Now arrange the circled letters to form the surprise answer, as suggested by the above cartoon.

Print answer here " ◯◯ - ◯◯◯◯◯◯ "

JUMBLE®

Unscramble these four Jumbles, one letter to each square, to form four ordinary words.

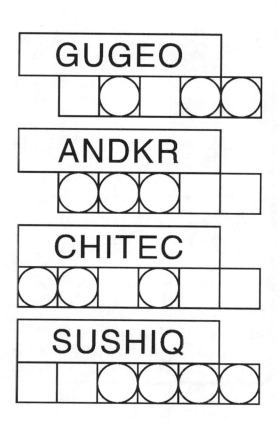

GUGEO

ANDKR

CHITEC

SUSHIQ

I have the spot picked out. I just need some investors.

You know I'll chip in!

SHE WANTED TO START HER OWN BREAD COMPANY AND PLANNED TO ---

Now arrange the circled letters to form the surprise answer, as suggested by the above cartoon.

Print answer here

JUMBLE®

Unscramble these four Jumbles, one letter
to each square, to form four ordinary words.

KARME

OBATO

TNUGIO

AEQURS

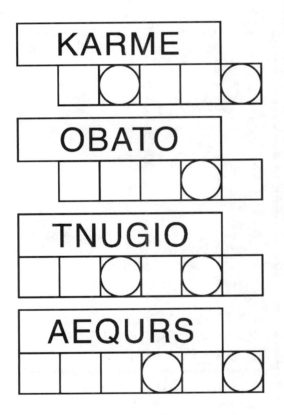

Well, he did it again.

This has got to stop! The paper is not cheap!

WHEN IT CAME TO DESTROYING
THE MORNING NEWSPAPER,
THEIR DOG WAS ---

Now arrange the circled letters
to form the surprise answer, as
suggested by the above cartoon.

Print answer here

JUMBLE®

Unscramble these four Jumbles, one letter to each square, to form four ordinary words.

LYUGL

DAAPN

MLUFEB

YAAAPP

Don't even think about it!

WHEN FACED WITH DANGER, THE MOTHER BIRD WAS ---

Now arrange the circled letters to form the surprise answer, as suggested by the above cartoon.

Print answer here

PUZZLE 74

JUMBLE®

Unscramble these four Jumbles, one letter to each square, to form four ordinary words.

RUBLT

LOYLW

DADOLE

LPTSIN

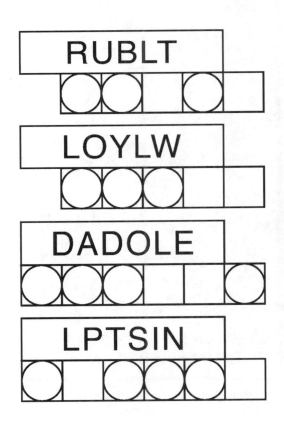

And here is 23, 24 and 25 bucks. You're rich!

I can't believe it!

You say that every week.

AFTER A SUCCESSFUL EVENING AT HER WEEKLY POKER GAME, SHE ENJOYED HER---

Now arrange the circled letters to form the surprise answer, as suggested by the above cartoon.

Print answer here "  " -

76

JUMBLE®

Unscramble these four Jumbles, one letter
to each square, to form four ordinary words.

VONWE

SFHER

DARPEA

LOYESL

Isn't she the cutest thing?

She's just amazing!

Aw!

She is special.

THE DEER HAD A BABY, AND
THEY JUST LOVED TO ---

Now arrange the circled letters
to form the surprise answer, as
suggested by the above cartoon.

**Print
answer
here**

JUMBLE®

Unscramble these four Jumbles, one letter to each square, to form four ordinary words.

LASLT

LYSET

ARNMLO

GNORTH

Awesome Audio

CALL NOW!

These are what you need! Then I can stop yelling at you.

What did you say?

WHEN THEY SAW THE COMMERCIAL FOR THE NEW HEARING AIDS, HIS WIFE WAS ---

Now arrange the circled letters to form the surprise answer, as suggested by the above cartoon.

Print answer here

JUMBLE®

Unscramble these four Jumbles, one letter to each square, to form four ordinary words.

RYEDB

ZIYZF

LANFIE

TUNOTB

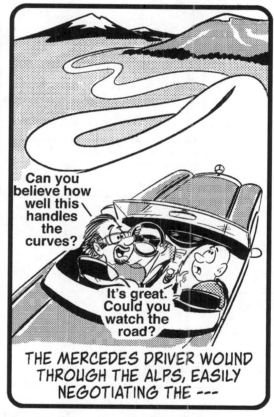

Can you believe how well this handles the curves?

It's great. Could you watch the road?

THE MERCEDES DRIVER WOUND THROUGH THE ALPS, EASILY NEGOTIATING THE ---

Now arrange the circled letters to form the surprise answer, as suggested by the above cartoon.

Print answer here

" ⃝⃝⃝⃝ " ⃝⃝ THE ⃝⃝⃝⃝

JUMBLE®

Unscramble these four Jumbles, one letter to each square, to form four ordinary words.

ORMGO

TARGN

VNLEEE

HRERCY

I dare each of you to give me a dozen! Betcha can't do it!

THE FARMER TALKED TO THE HENS AND LIKED TO ---

Now arrange the circled letters to form the surprise answer, as suggested by the above cartoon.

Print answer here

JUMBLE®

Unscramble these four Jumbles, one letter
to each square, to form four ordinary words.

UKQCA

NIFGL

DINERD

CEIETX

Wow! Great price. Why is it so cheap?

It's past its sell-by date. We need to get rid of it.

80% OFF!

HAPPY H₂O

THEY FOUND AN INVENTORY OF
OLD SPARKLING WATER AND
DECIDED IT SHOULD BE ---

Now arrange the circled letters
to form the surprise answer, as
suggested by the above cartoon.

Print
answer
here

81

JUMBLE®

Unscramble these four Jumbles, one letter to each square, to form four ordinary words.

SYEAS

LUCKA

TECOPI

LIEMWD

Enjoy my chips.

I can't hear you. I'm too busy counting them.

We can't beat you tonight.

WHEN COMPARED TO HIS COMPETITION, THE POKER PLAYER ---

Now arrange the circled letters to form the surprise answer, as suggested by the above cartoon.

Print answer here

JUMBLE®

Unscramble these four Jumbles, one letter
to each square, to form four ordinary words.

RFMOU

CIPER

XSSEEC

TBEANU

I'm almost finished with the beef chapter.

Ooh! Let's have that recipe for dinner!

THE ORIGINAL VERSION OF
HER COOKBOOK WAS A ---

Now arrange the circled letters
to form the surprise answer, as
suggested by the above cartoon.

Print answer here " ◯◯◯◯◯◯◯◯◯◯ "

JUMBLE®

Unscramble these four Jumbles, one letter
to each square, to form four ordinary words.

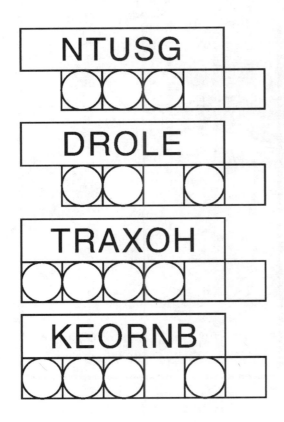

NTUSG

DROLE

TRAXOH

KEORNB

Problems with your shotgun?

Nothing I couldn't handle. It should work properly now.

PULL

SHE WAS ABLE TO FIX
HER OWN SKEET GUN
BECAUSE SHE WAS A ---

Now arrange the circled letters
to form the surprise answer, as
suggested by the above cartoon.

Print
answer
here

JUMBLE®

Unscramble these four Jumbles, one letter
to each square, to form four ordinary words.

VALEG

KAYLE

FLABEF

SRUPEU

I can't
even see
the green.

Just hit
it in that
direction.

THE 600-YARD PAR 5
WAS THE LONGEST HOLE
ON THE COURSE ---

Now arrange the circled letters
to form the surprise answer, as
suggested by the above cartoon.

Print answer here

JUMBLE®

Unscramble these four Jumbles, one letter to each square, to form four ordinary words.

NROPE

AZUEG

AUNAGI

HRETIM

It's so windy I don't think we're going to make it on schedule.

I guess we'll get there when we get there.

A FLOCK OF GEESE WAS HEADED SOUTH FOR THE WINTER, BUT WHEN THEY'D ARRIVE WAS ---

Now arrange the circled letters to form the surprise answer, as suggested by the above cartoon.

Print answer here

JUMBLE®

Unscramble these four Jumbles, one letter to each square, to form four ordinary words.

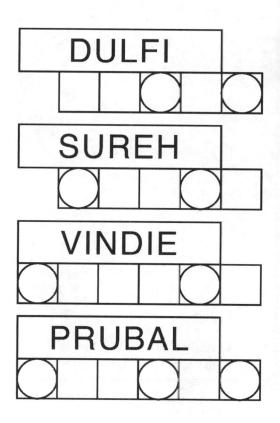

DULFI

SUREH

VINDIE

PRUBAL

You look warm.

I am. It's getting colder.

Hope you have plenty for me.

FIREWOOD FOR SALE

IT WAS COLD OUTSIDE, SO THE FIREWOOD SALESMAN ---

Now arrange the circled letters to form the surprise answer, as suggested by the above cartoon.

Print answer here

JUMBLE®

Unscramble these four Jumbles, one letter to each square, to form four ordinary words.

GFROO

DUYPG

RUBWOR

NITMYU

Was our farm always this big?

Your grandfather started with only a few acres and kept buying more land.

THEIR FAMILY FARM HAD BEEN BUILT ---

Now arrange the circled letters to form the surprise answer, as suggested by the above cartoon.

Print answer here ⬜⬜⬜⬜ **THE** ⬜⬜⬜⬜⬜⬜ ⬜⬜

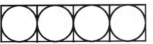

JUMBLE®

Unscramble these four Jumbles, one letter to each square, to form four ordinary words.

CLUEN
◯◯◯

SALOS
◯◯◯

RPTIEM
◯◯◯◯

FRYRUL
◯◯◯

WHEN MICHELANGELO WAS ASKED IF HE COULD CREATE A MARBLE STATUE, HE SAID ---

Now arrange the circled letters to form the surprise answer, as suggested by the above cartoon.

Print answer here " ◯◯◯◯◯◯◯ - ◯◯◯◯ "

JUMBLE®

Unscramble these four Jumbles, one letter
to each square, to form four ordinary words.

CUTHH

NAYML

ITTCEK

CROOTD

We're not
getting
anywhere
like this.

These
leaves are
tough!

THEY TRIED USING
MACHETES TO CUT
THEIR WAY THROUGH
THE JUNGLE, BUT ---

Now arrange the circled letters
to form the surprise answer, as
suggested by the above cartoon.

*Print
answer
here*

◯◯◯◯◯◯◯ ' ◯   ◯◯◯◯◯   ◯◯

JUMBLE®

Unscramble these four Jumbles, one letter
to each square, to form four ordinary words.

RVOPE

SYATT

RSAYGS

LDFIED

I think we have
enough for a taxi
to the airport.

We should
have gone to
the beach.

CASINOS ON THE "STRIP"
MAKE SO MUCH MONEY
BECAUSE LOTS OF
PEOPLE GO TO ---

Now arrange the circled letters
to form the surprise answer, as
suggested by the above cartoon.

Print
answer
here

" ◯◯◯◯ " ◯◯◯◯◯

JUMBLE®

Unscramble these four Jumbles, one letter to each square, to form four ordinary words.

OPRGU

WLIHR

PXOEES

NTAEEG

He acts like such an alpha male.

He has so much confidence in his stride.

WHEN THE DOG MOVED HIS TAIL BACK AND FORTH WHILE WALKING, THEY COMMENTED ON HIS ---

Now arrange the circled letters to form the surprise answer, as suggested by the above cartoon.

Print answer here

JUMBLE®

Unscramble these four Jumbles, one letter to each square, to form four ordinary words.

KAHIK

LICLH

SERUSD

SFIENU

He's here to help us!

Thank you!

WHEN THE JEEP RAN OFF THE ROAD, THE GIRAFFE WAS WILLING TO ---

Now arrange the circled letters to form the surprise answer, as suggested by the above cartoon.

Print answer here

JUMBLE®

Unscramble these four Jumbles, one letter to each square, to form four ordinary words.

RITDH

NILTF

RYAMLW

THOSEO

Hey! Why no toupee?

I want to swim and enjoy myself while we're here.

THE MAN USUALLY WORE A TOUPEE, BUT WHEN HE RELAXED, HE COULD ---

Now arrange the circled letters to form the surprise answer, as suggested by the above cartoon.

Print answer here

JUMBLE®

Unscramble these four Jumbles, one letter
to each square, to form four ordinary words.

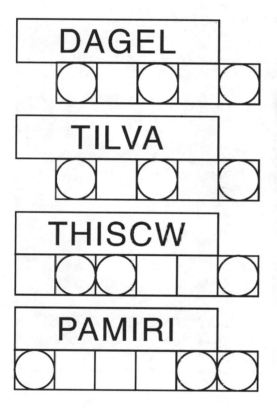

DAGEL

TILVA

THISCW

PAMIRI

I can't
wait to
see this
in action.

I can't wait to
wear a clean
shirt.

Will
Bunny
get
dizzy?

THE NEW WASHING MACHINE
HAD JUST ARRIVED AND
THEY WERE READY TO ---

Now arrange the circled letters
to form the surprise answer, as
suggested by the above cartoon.

Print answer here

 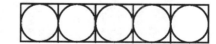

JUMBLE®

Unscramble these four Jumbles, one letter to each square, to form four ordinary words.

LIGUT

AZPAL

PHOYCP

PORCIT

I'm glad we were all able to work together on making this.

We need to celebrate like this more often.

IF LAWMAKERS WORKED TOGETHER, THEY COULD CELEBRATE WITH A ---

Now arrange the circled letters to form the surprise answer, as suggested by the above cartoon.

Print answer here

JUMBLE®

Unscramble these four Jumbles, one letter to each square, to form four ordinary words.

LEHOL

FLUBF

WAMEOD

RARBHO

THE GODFATHER
MARLON BRANDO
AL PACINO

If we can't get a ticket, I know the manager. He owes me a favor.

I hope we can get in.

WHEN "THE GODFATHER" PREMIERED IN 1972, THEATERS WERE ---

Now arrange the circled letters to form the surprise answer, as suggested by the above cartoon.

Print answer here

JUMBLE®

Unscramble these four Jumbles, one letter to each square, to form four ordinary words.

NTEGA

POSYU

RRTIWE

NAEEGG

The new workers are costing us more than we're making.

Our profits are hurting because of this.

THE WINDOW COMPANY WAS STRUGGLING AND EXPERIENCING ---

Now arrange the circled letters to form the surprise answer, as suggested by the above cartoon.

Print answer here

"   "

JUMBLE®

Unscramble these four Jumbles, one letter to each square, to form four ordinary words.

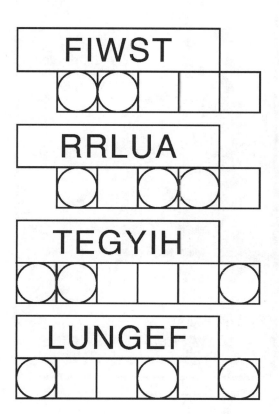

FIWST

RRLUA

TEGYIH

LUNGEF

This lighter isn't working again.

You can always count on matches to light.

WHEN IT COMES TO LIGHTING A CANDLE, USING MATCHES IS USUALLY A ---

Now arrange the circled letters to form the surprise answer, as suggested by the above cartoon.

Print answer here

JUMBLE®

Unscramble these four Jumbles, one letter to each square, to form four ordinary words.

SOHEW

PUCEO

TURGET

DXEOTU

Is everything all right? Do we need to call the doctor?

No. I'm fine. I'm just tired. Just like the doctor said I would be.

SHE WAS HAVING TWINS AND WAS EXPERIENCING ALL THE THINGS SHE ---

Now arrange the circled letters to form the surprise answer, as suggested by the above cartoon.

Print answer here

" "

JUMBLE®

Unscramble these four Jumbles, one letter
to each square, to form four ordinary words.

GACYE

SNATL

THELEM

LRIDEV

We need to
head into
Bangor for
some lobster
rolls.

There are
so many
great
places to
rent here.

LODGING IS IMPORTANT
TO THE ECONOMY OF THE
"PINE TREE STATE" AND
IS CONSIDERED A ---

Now arrange the circled letters
to form the surprise answer, as
suggested by the above cartoon.

Print
answer
here

" ◯◯◯◯◯ - ◯◯◯◯ "

JUMBLE®

Unscramble these four Jumbles, one letter
to each square, to form four ordinary words.

DOLFO

NOTRF

MANYFI

XUDLEE

Should we wake him up before he gets too far away?

Nah. We'll keep an eye on him.

WHEN HE FELL ASLEEP ON THE INNER TUBE, HE ---

Now arrange the circled letters
to form the surprise answer, as
suggested by the above cartoon.

Print
answer
here

JUMBLE®

Unscramble these four Jumbles, one letter
to each square, to form four ordinary words.

PNTIU

TOOPH

GLIWYG

NCRABH

So this will
heat the house?

Don't
touch that!
You may
get burned.

AFTER THE PLUMBER MADE
ALL THE CONNECTIONS TO
THE BOILER, THE RADIATORS
WERE ---

Now arrange the circled letters
to form the surprise answer, as
suggested by the above cartoon.

*Print
answer
here*

103

JUMBLE®

Unscramble these four Jumbles, one letter
to each square, to form four ordinary words.

SEQTU

FADRU

DRAFIA

GENUBE

Here you go.
That will be $8.

Wow! Only
$8? That's a
great price.
Look, it's the
New Year's
Eve ball!

Total $8

THE PRICE SHE PAID FOR
AN NYC CAB RIDE TO 45TH
AND BROADWAY WAS ---

Now arrange the circled letters
to form the surprise answer, as
suggested by the above cartoon.

**Print
answer
here**

" ◯◯◯◯◯ " ◯◯◯ ◯◯◯◯◯◯◯

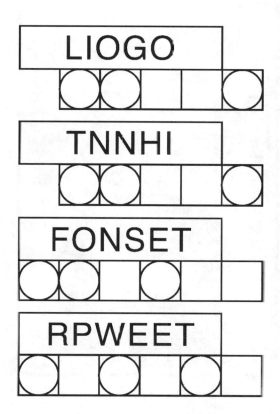

JUMBLE

Unscramble these four Jumbles, one letter to each square, to form four ordinary words.

LIOGO

TNNHI

FONSET

RPWEET

This one connects to an app, right? I really want a good scale.

That's the latest model.

BEFORE DECIDING ON WHICH NEW SCALE TO PURCHASE, SHE WANTED TO ---

Now arrange the circled letters to form the surprise answer, as suggested by the above cartoon.

Print answer here ⬡⬡⬡⬡⬡ **HER** ⬡⬡⬡⬡⬡⬡⬡⬡

JUMBLE®

Unscramble these four Jumbles, one letter to each square, to form four ordinary words.

ANSRL

DURED

RATEKM

YBHUCB

That idiot was on his phone and not paying attention.

Ridiculous.

HE DIDN'T LOOK IN HIS REARVIEW MIRROR BEFORE BACKING UP AND AS A RESULT WAS ---

Now arrange the circled letters to form the surprise answer, as suggested by the above cartoon.

Print answer here

JUMBLE®

Unscramble these four Jumbles, one letter to each square, to form four ordinary words.

VDITO

NAYHD

NARMAT

NEYRTS

This is the debut of this model!

This will help my bookkeeping.

I can't wait to give it a try.

WHEN THE NEW ABACUS CAME OUT, CUSTOMERS WERE READY TO ---

Now arrange the circled letters to form the surprise answer, as suggested by the above cartoon.

Print answer here

 "  "

JUMBLE®

Unscramble these four Jumbles, one letter to each square, to form four ordinary words.

MOCPH

TOHTO

GLIGEJ

BAIEEN

I'll be right with you! Be ready to work!

He's the best!

I'm on his waiting list.

I am!

JAMES WAS VERY BUSY AS A PERSONAL TRAINER WITH SO MANY PEOPLE ---

Now arrange the circled letters to form the surprise answer, as suggested by the above cartoon.

Print answer here

JUMBLE®

Unscramble these four Jumbles, one letter
to each square, to form four ordinary words.

ETXRE

CERFO

ASMCUP

ONKVIE

Today's Guest JUMBLER is
DENNIS the MENACE

FOR DENNIS, FINDING
ROOM FOR DESSERT
WAS A ---

Now arrange the circled letters
to form the surprise answer, as
suggested by the above cartoon.

**Print
answer
here**

 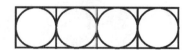

JUMBLE®

Unscramble these four Jumbles, one letter
to each square, to form four ordinary words.

LIYFL

NITEW

TRFGOO

CAPUTE

Today's Guest JUMBLER is
DAN McCONNELL
MAD Magazine Cartoonist

SWITCH IT OFF!

BZZT
BZZT
BZZT

THE EXPERIENCE OF USING HIS
FIRST BATTERY-OPERATED
TOOTHBRUSH WAS ---

Now arrange the circled letters
to form the surprise answer, as
suggested by the above cartoon.

**Print
answer
here**

JUMBLE®

Unscramble these four Jumbles, one letter to each square, to form four ordinary words.

SOEGO

VOSEH

GLUNEO

VITREH

Today's Guest JUMBLER is
JOHN HAMBROCK
Creator of The Brilliant Mind of Edison Lee

ONCE IT'S ALOFT, IT'LL BE VISIBLE FOR MILES!

He

EDISON FILLED HIS ATTIC WITH HELIUM BECAUSE HE WANTED A ----

Now arrange the circled letters to form the surprise answer, as suggested by the above cartoon.

Print answer here

JUMBLE®

Unscramble these four Jumbles, one letter to each square, to form four ordinary words.

ORTFN

TRIDH

JCEBTO

SNAFET

Today's Guest JUMBLER is
LINCOLN PEIRCE
Creator of BIG NATE

WRITE THAT ONE HUNDRED TIMES.

I will not draw comics in class.

WHEN NATE HAD TO STAY AFTER SCHOOL, HE WAS ---

Now arrange the circled letters to form the surprise answer, as suggested by the above cartoon.

Print answer here

" ☐☐☐☐☐ " ☐☐☐☐☐

JUMBLE®

Unscramble these four Jumbles, one letter
to each square, to form four ordinary words.

SROCS

CNPHI

NNSEKU

TEPRYO

Today's Guest JUMBLER is
SCOTT HILBURN
Creator of THE ARGYLE SWEATER

I'LL SELL YOU THE CHEVYS
BUT I'M KEEPING THE FORD.

Ford

AFTER SELLING ALMOST ALL
OF HIS PICKUPS, THE
HORSE WAS A - - -

Now arrange the circled letters
to form the surprise answer, as
suggested by the above cartoon.

**Print
answer
here**

⬡⬡⬡ " ⬡⬡⬡⬡⬡ " ⬡⬡⬡⬡

JUMBLE®

Unscramble these four Jumbles, one letter to each square, to form four ordinary words.

ANIPO

LIRTL

NECCTA

NOTLAA

Today's Guest JUMBLERS are
Bunny Hoest & John Reiner
Creators of THE LOCKHORNS

"LORETTA'S VOICE HAS AN ARRESTING QUALITY. IT MAKES YOU WANT TO ..."

Now arrange the circled letters to form the surprise answer, as suggested by the above cartoon.

Print answer here ⬡⬡⬡⬡ **THE** ⬡⬡⬡⬡⬡⬡

JUMBLE®

Unscramble these four Jumbles, one letter to each square, to form four ordinary words.

CMIMI

CUPHO

NOYELL

VIRRDE

Okay, okay! You win!

Growing up, he never let me win either.

You're next, brother.

THE TEEN ARM WRESTLED HIS DAD'S BROTHER UNTIL THE TEEN ---

Now arrange the circled letters to form the surprise answer, as suggested by the above cartoon.

Print answer here

  !

JUMBLE®

Unscramble these four Jumbles, one letter to each square, to form four ordinary words.

TIFHA

PHEDT

SCEEUX

NLODYF

I love you from the bottom of my heart.

You're just buttering me up.

YOU COULD TELL THAT THE LOBSTERS WERE IN LOVE BY THEIR ---

Now arrange the circled letters to form the surprise answer, as suggested by the above cartoon.

Print answer here

JUMBLE®

Unscramble these four Jumbles, one letter to each square, to form four ordinary words.

BLERE

NYILV

TODIUS

OGLNOA

We've got this, honey.

What do you mean "we"? I'm doing all the work!

Keep pushing. You're doing a great job.

HAVING A BABY CAN BE A LOT OF WORK BECAUSE IT'S ---

Now arrange the circled letters to form the surprise answer, as suggested by the above cartoon.

Print answer here

JUMBLE®

Unscramble these four Jumbles, one letter to each square, to form four ordinary words.

EEOSB

LIVAL

WOCARD

PRISTI

I'm heading out. Are you leaving?

Not until I figure this out.

HE'D FAILED TO FIGURE OUT THE SOLUTION BUT WASN'T GIVING UP BECAUSE OF HIS---

Now arrange the circled letters to form the surprise answer, as suggested by the above cartoon.

Print answer here

JUMBLE®

Unscramble these four Jumbles, one letter to each square, to form four ordinary words.

ENHOY

LRIEN

PLUCTS

CAJEKT

It's very simple. This acorn will grow into an oak tree.

That little thing?

ACORN=OAK TREE

ACORNS TURN INTO OAK TREES. THAT'S THE EXPLANATION ---

Now arrange the circled letters to form the surprise answer, as suggested by the above cartoon.

Print answer here

JUMBLE®

Unscramble these four Jumbles, one letter to each square, to form four ordinary words.

HARNC

MYTEH

MRISEM

ENNBIG

I can't believe how nice this place is. And those views!

There's not a better place for a drink in Chicago.

WHEN THEY PUT A COCKTAIL LOUNGE ON THE 96TH FLOOR OF THE HANCOCK, THEY ---

Now arrange the circled letters to form the surprise answer, as suggested by the above cartoon.

Print answer here

 THE

JUMBLE

Unscramble these four Jumbles, one letter to each square, to form four ordinary words.

ANIYR

EEGVR

SREYDS

PTIEOT

Will you look at that! You all must have been very good this year.

It's the most amazing thing I've ever seen!

It's beautiful!

THE KIDS AWOKE TO FIND GIFTS UNDER THE TREE AND LOVED THE WAY THEY WERE ---

Now arrange the circled letters to form the surprise answer, as suggested by the above cartoon.

Print answer here

JUMBLE®

Unscramble these four Jumbles, one letter
to each square, to form four ordinary words.

PMILE

WARNP

BELVAR

NTEEDO

In the money again!

He sure can run!—

Who needs a job when we have you?

THE HORSE THAT WON LOTS
OF MONEY FOR HIS OWNERS
WAS A THOROUGH ---

Now arrange the circled letters
to form the surprise answer, as
suggested by the above cartoon.

Print
answer
here

" ⭘⭘⭘⭘ " ⭘⭘⭘⭘⭘⭘

JUMBLE®

Unscramble these four Jumbles, one letter to each square, to form four ordinary words.

UAOTQ

CANTE

LOCLRS

BLYAFB

Let's cross the street.

Eww!

THEY SAW THE POLLUTED AIR BY THE SMOKING SECTION AND DECIDED TO ---

Now arrange the circled letters to form the surprise answer, as suggested by the above cartoon.

Print answer here

JUMBLE®

Unscramble these four Jumbles, one letter to each square, to form four ordinary words.

RUENT

GENIT

BLLOGA

WOSIND

We're kind of anxious to get the story. Will you be done soon?

I'm almost finished.

WHEN ASKED WHEN HE'D BE DONE WRITING HIS NEW SHORT STORY, THE AUTHOR SAID ---

Now arrange the circled letters to form the surprise answer, as suggested by the above cartoon.

Print answer here

⬜⬜ ⬜⬜⬜'⬜ ⬜⬜ ⬜⬜⬜⬜

JUMBLE®

Unscramble these four Jumbles, one letter to each square, to form four ordinary words.

MOSPT

NRIBE

ROSMYT

CANGLE

They have been at the same spot for years.

They work so well together.

THE MIMES HAD WORKED TOGETHER FOR YEARS AND ENJOYED BEING ---

Now arrange the circled letters to form the surprise answer, as suggested by the above cartoon.

Print answer here

JUMBLE®

Unscramble these four Jumbles, one letter to each square, to form four ordinary words.

VYRAG

PIWRE

FEXRIP

NABREN

WHEN HE PROPOSED TO HER ON DECEMBER 31, THEY WERE ABLE TO ---

Now arrange the circled letters to form the surprise answer, as suggested by the above cartoon.

Print answer here ⬡⬡⬡⬡ IN THE ⬡⬡⬡ ⬡⬡⬡⬡

126

JUMBLE®

Unscramble these four Jumbles, one letter to each square, to form four ordinary words.

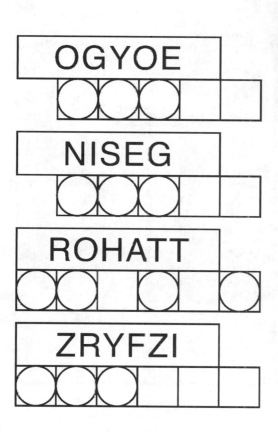

OGYOE

NISEG

ROHATT

ZRYFZI

He has his goals set.

He's doing everything he can to have his chance.

THERE WAS NO GUARANTEE HE COULD BECOME AN NBA PLAYER, BUT HE WAS ---

Now arrange the circled letters to form the surprise answer, as suggested by the above cartoon.

Print answer here

JUMBLE®

Unscramble these four Jumbles, one letter to each square, to form four ordinary words.

ROYSR

VAHYE

CODAIZ

RITEAD

You're insane! Put that on! It will save your life, and it's the law!

Why does it bug you so much? I've never worn one and I never will.

HE REFUSED TO WEAR HIS SEAT BELT WHEN BEHIND THE WHEEL, AND THAT ---

Now arrange the circled letters to form the surprise answer, as suggested by the above cartoon.

Print answer here

JUMBLE®

Unscramble these four Jumbles, one letter to each square, to form four ordinary words.

RYOWR

NOYHE

GLEPTI

STARGI

The dam was built to last. It will generate energy for generations to come.

My parents took me here when I was a kid. It hasn't changed.

THE HOOVER DAM HYDROELECTRIC FACILITY, BUILT IN THE '30S, HAS PROVEN ITS ---

Now arrange the circled letters to form the surprise answer, as suggested by the above cartoon.

Print answer here

JUMBLE®

Unscramble these four Jumbles, one letter to each square, to form four ordinary words.

OWSNO

UVNEE

RAYTAS

DUROAN

This farmer has made good money on billboards.

He wants more.

JUMBLETOWN 10
CAPITAL CITY 30

THE BILLBOARDS WERE SO PROFITABLE, THEY DECIDED TO ---

Now arrange the circled letters to form the surprise answer, as suggested by the above cartoon.

Print answer here

" ☐☐ " ☐ ☐☐☐☐ ☐☐☐

JUMBLE®

Unscramble these four Jumbles, one letter to each square, to form four ordinary words.

WONNK

RWODL

CAAUBS

CITKEP

They sure make it easy.

They love coming here.

WITH THE DOGS GETTING ALONG SO WELL TOGETHER, GOING FOR A STROLL WAS A ---

Now arrange the circled letters to form the surprise answer, as suggested by the above cartoon.

Print answer here

THE

JUMBLE®

Unscramble these four Jumbles, one letter to each square, to form four ordinary words.

RUYBL

CAXTE

OENDOW

CCLEKA

Earth's layers

There you go! Great answer!

It's as hot as the surface of the sun.

IF YOU THOUGHT EARTH'S CENTER COULD REACH 10,000 DEGREES FAHRENHEIT, YOU'D ---

Now arrange the circled letters to form the surprise answer, as suggested by the above cartoon.

Print answer here

◯◯ " ◯◯◯◯ - ◯◯◯ "

JUMBLE

Unscramble these four Jumbles, one letter
to each square, to form four ordinary words.

NUYRN

GEHED

TIDYDO

PESEYL

First we miss
our flight. Now
I have to pay
for this?

This
was the
only
room
left.

It has
two
toilets.

THE HOTEL ROOM WAS
EXPENSIVE AND THEY HAD
NO CHOICE BUT TO ---

Now arrange the circled letters
to form the surprise answer, as
suggested by the above cartoon.

**Print
answer
here** ⬡⬡⬡⬡⬡ **THE** ⬡⬡⬡⬡⬡

JUMBLE®

Unscramble these four Jumbles, one letter to each square, to form four ordinary words.

URROM

MUYTM

SHOOYC

TANETB

No one out here can keep up. I'm thinking of getting more horsepower.

You don't say.

He never stops.

THE GUY WHO WOULDN'T STOP TALKING ABOUT HOW FAST HIS BOAT COULD GO WAS A ---

Now arrange the circled letters to form the surprise answer, as suggested by the above cartoon.

Print answer here

JUMBLE®

Unscramble these four Jumbles, one letter to each square, to form four ordinary words.

ZAAEM

RFETA

NYHHEP

CROUNC

We shall honor Pheidippides and his run from Marathon to Athens with a competition of the same distance.

I better start training.

Can people run that far?

RUNNING A MARATHON WAS INVENTED BY THE ---

Now arrange the circled letters to form the surprise answer, as suggested by the above cartoon.

Print answer here

135

JUMBLE®

Unscramble these four Jumbles, one letter
to each square, to form four ordinary words.

GOYFG

AYNNN

LWSOYL

TPTIEE

Construction began in
1869. The first
steel-wire suspension
bridge took 14 years
to build.

Wow, that's
old.

THE BROOKLYN BRIDGE IS
ONE OF THE OLDEST OF
ITS KIND, THANKS TO ITS ---

Now arrange the circled letters
to form the surprise answer, as
suggested by the above cartoon.

Print
answer
here

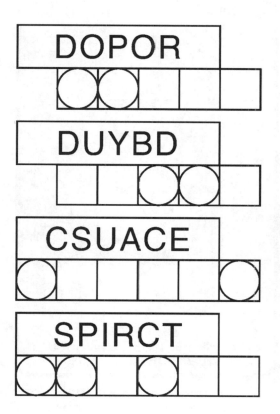

JUMBLE®

Unscramble these four Jumbles, one letter to each square, to form four ordinary words.

DOPOR

DUYBD

CSUACE

SPIRCT

I can't shuffle this mess.

This deck is trashed.

Toss those. I found a new deck.

THE DECK USED BY THE POKER PLAYERS WAS OLD. THEY ALL AGREED IT SHOULD BE ---

Now arrange the circled letters to form the surprise answer, as suggested by the above cartoon.

Print answer here

PUZZLE 136

JUMBLE®

Unscramble these four Jumbles, one letter to each square, to form four ordinary words.

FIDTR

FINKE

KEREAU

LWOOLH

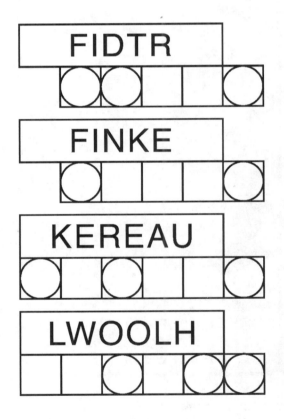

I can't believe we are realtors just like mom was.

It's the family business.

Family Home Realty

SOLD

WHEN THE SISTERS STARTED A BUSINESS TOGETHER, MUCH OF WHAT THEY DID WAS ---

Now arrange the circled letters to form the surprise answer, as suggested by the above cartoon.

Print answer here

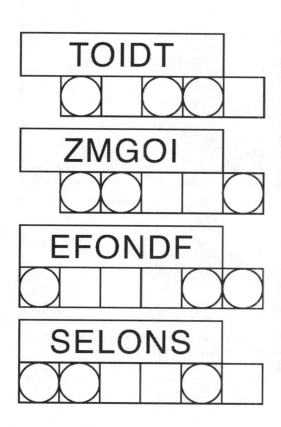

JUMBLE®

Unscramble these four Jumbles, one letter to each square, to form four ordinary words.

TOIDT

ZMGOI

EFONDF

SELONS

You did it!

Finally! I've wanted to reach this hole in two shots for years.

SHE FINALLY REACHED THE PAR 5 IN TWO SHOTS AFTER SHE ---

Now arrange the circled letters to form the surprise answer, as suggested by the above cartoon.

Print answer here

JUMBLE®

Unscramble these four Jumbles, one letter to each square, to form four ordinary words.

USETG

ENESS

PIHEIP

FRUGIE

CONSTELLATION PRIZE
ASTROLOGY REA...S.

Hey! I'm a Leo!

That's good! I see great things for you.

IN ORDER TO ATTRACT CUSTOMERS, THE ASTROLOGER ---

Now arrange the circled letters to form the surprise answer, as suggested by the above cartoon.

Print answer here

JUMBLE®

Unscramble these four Jumbles, one letter
to each square, to form four ordinary words.

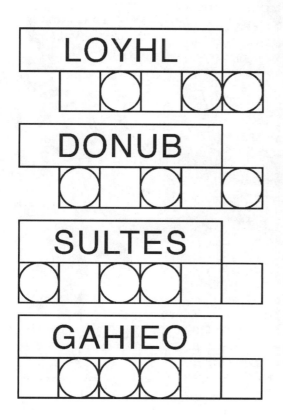

LOYHL

DONUB

SULTES

GAHIEO

Thanks for
being such
a great
customer.

I can't believe
this is the final
time I'll be pur-
chasing from
you.

These are
a bargain.

It's a
shame
she's
closing.

LAST DAY
TODAY

THE STORE WAS CLOSING,
AND LOYAL CUSTOMERS
CAME IN ON THE FINAL
DAY FOR THE ---

Now arrange the circled letters
to form the surprise answer, as
suggested by the above cartoon.

**Print
answer
here**

" - " "

141

JUMBLE®

Unscramble these four Jumbles, one letter to each square, to form four ordinary words.

MOAAR

CFARS

EDITEC

MUEHAN

Our fans are going crazy for you.

They don't even know my name.

They do now.

FOR RINGO, REPLACING PETE BEST AS THE BEATLES' DRUMMER ---

Now arrange the circled letters to form the surprise answer, as suggested by the above cartoon.

Print answer here

◯◯◯◯ ◯◯◯ ◯ "◯◯◯◯◯◯"

JUMBLE®

Unscramble these four Jumbles, one letter
to each square, to form four ordinary words.

XONTI

GALEE

DMTOEH

SRYUTT

CANDIDATE JONES ARRESTED
BREAKING NEWS

I can't believe this. I quit!

JONES ☆
Just when I was starting to like the guy.

How could he do this to us?

WHEN THE POLITICIAN WAS
ARRESTED FOR CORRUPTION,
HIS SUPPORTERS ---

Now arrange the circled letters
to form the surprise answer, as
suggested by the above cartoon.

Print
answer
here

  OF "  "

JUMBLE®

Unscramble these four Jumbles, one letter to each square, to form four ordinary words.

RNBDA

GLOMU

GOINNG

PRUTIN

Here are the keys. Better get going. We'll be there in a little bit.

Honey, I'm afraid Bear might slow me down.

Mommy, Bear wants to marathon with you.

I ♥ JUMBLE

ON THE MORNING OF THE MARATHON, SHE NEEDED TO BE ---

Now arrange the circled letters to form the surprise answer, as suggested by the above cartoon.

Print answer here

JUMBLE®

Unscramble these four Jumbles, one letter to each square, to form four ordinary words.

NEAYH

VAWIE

TIBETR

BREGLI

It has that new-justice smell. Bring in the first case.

Here we go!

THE COURTROOM WAS BRAND-NEW, AND THE JUDGE WAS READY TO ---

Now arrange the circled letters to form the surprise answer, as suggested by the above cartoon.

Print answer here

JUMBLE®

Unscramble these four Jumbles, one letter
to each square, to form four ordinary words.

LOFRO

KASYH

TONUDL

ISIMTF

So,
how
does it
look?

Wow! I didn't
think it would
work. Looking
good, honey!

AFTER SEEING HOW WELL HIS
HAIR TRANSPLANT TURNED
OUT, HIS WIFE SAID ---

Now arrange the circled letters
to form the surprise answer, as
suggested by the above cartoon.

**Print
answer
here**

JUMBLE®

Unscramble these four Jumbles, one letter
to each square, to form four ordinary words.

MOTPE

WKONN

LBOWBE

DMEUTI

It turned out
perfect, Nick!

I love
mahogany!
It always
comes out
looking like
a million
bucks!

THE TABLE MADE OUT OF
MAHOGANY WAS PERFECT,
JUST LIKE HE ---

Now arrange the circled letters
to form the surprise answer, as
suggested by the above cartoon.

*Print
answer
here*

JUMBLE®

Unscramble these four Jumbles, one letter
to each square, to form four ordinary words.

ELTFE

PZATO

NXADPE

DIRMEL

Help us raise funds

$

The clock thanks you for your help.

It's always been there for me. I've never been late.

SAVE THE CLOCK

IT REQUIRED FIXING, SO
THEY HELPED REPAIR THE
TOWN CLOCK IN ITS ---

Now arrange the circled letters
to form the surprise answer, as
suggested by the above cartoon.

Print answer here

JUMBLE®

Unscramble these four Jumbles, one letter to each square, to form four ordinary words.

NOPER

LICDH

GLIMEN

RFAOLL

Who are you writing?

I'm reaching out to Dennis. We haven't been in touch since our last fishing trip.

HE WROTE A LETTER TO HIS OLD FISHING BUDDY BECAUSE HE WANTED TO ---

Now arrange the circled letters to form the surprise answer, as suggested by the above cartoon.

Print answer here

◯◯◯◯◯ ◯◯◯ A ◯◯◯◯◯

JUMBLE®

Unscramble these four Jumbles, one letter to each square, to form four ordinary words.

NOONI

NIMCE

RPMEET

RWHOGT

I hope she'll have a long reign.

It's her time.

FOR ELIZABETH, BECOMING QUEEN OF ENGLAND IN 1952 WAS A ---

Now arrange the circled letters to form the surprise answer, as suggested by the above cartoon.

Print answer here

JUMBLE®

Unscramble these four Jumbles, one letter to each square, to form four ordinary words.

GNIES

SAYID

WNTIHI

VLARFO

I have a house I need to be framing. Let's get a move on!

THE CARPENTER WAS STUCK IN TRAFFIC INSTEAD OF ---

Now arrange the circled letters to form the surprise answer, as suggested by the above cartoon.

Print answer here

JUMBLE®

Unscramble these four Jumbles, one letter to each square, to form four ordinary words.

ZUGEA

TIARO

NMMTOE

SMOCIA

Here are the entrees.

I love dinner at the club.

Great! I'm hungry after that round.

I love their club sand-wiches.

WHEN THEY DINED IN THE CLUBHOUSE AFTER A ROUND OF GOLF, THEY ENJOYED THE ---

Now arrange the circled letters to form the surprise answer, as suggested by the above cartoon.

Print answer here

JUMBLE®

Unscramble these four Jumbles, one letter
to each square, to form four ordinary words.

UDHMI

MOXIA

GOTOES

GLAUPE

Oh, yay. I
don't think
I'm hungry
anymore.

Look
who's
here.

WHEN SHE SAW HER FORMER
HUSBAND IN THE RESTAURANT,
SHE WASN'T ---

Now arrange the circled letters
to form the surprise answer, as
suggested by the above cartoon.

Print
answer
here

" ⬡⬡ - ⬡⬡⬡⬡⬡⬡⬡⬡ "

153

JUMBLE®

Unscramble these four Jumbles, one letter to each square, to form four ordinary words.

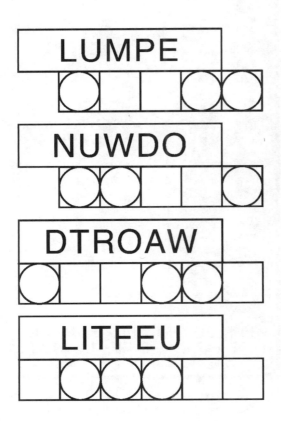

LUMPE

NUWDO

DTROAW

LITFEU

Didn't I tell you this would be nice?

Yes. I guess you're right. It is pretty nice.

HE DIDN'T INITIALLY LOVE THE IDEA OF BUYING THE WOOD STOVE, BUT HE ---

Now arrange the circled letters to form the surprise answer, as suggested by the above cartoon.

Print answer here

JUMBLE®

Unscramble these four Jumbles, one letter to each square, to form four ordinary words.

MBUOJ

ODESU

TRYPET

CINLPE

I'm done with this darn computer.

Whoa! Did you try restarting it?

THE GUY WHO WASN'T TECH-SAVVY GOT SO FRUSTRATED WITH HIS COMPUTER THAT HE ---

Now arrange the circled letters to form the surprise answer, as suggested by the above cartoon.

Print answer here

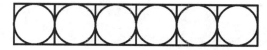

JUMBLE®

Unscramble these four Jumbles, one letter to each square, to form four ordinary words.

MCAPH

NERDT

LOOIER

SNSITI

Cut! Can we quickly do it again but with your arms out straighter?

Sure. The lasers are put in later, right?

THE DURATION BETWEEN THE FIRST AND SECOND TAKE WOULD DEPEND ON THE ---

Now arrange the circled letters to form the surprise answer, as suggested by the above cartoon.

Print answer here

" ◯◯ - ◯◯◯◯◯◯◯ " ◯◯◯◯◯

JUMBLE®

Unscramble these four Jumbles, one letter to each square, to form four ordinary words.

MPETT

FOYLT

SOONPI

WARELY

I think we did a lot of damage.

Not a dime left in our budget. I'm exhausted.

AFTER A LONG DAY OF SHOPPING, THE ROOMMATES CAME HOME ---

Now arrange the circled letters to form the surprise answer, as suggested by the above cartoon.

Print answer here

JUMBLE®

Unscramble these four Jumbles, one letter
to each square, to form four ordinary words.

TAAEB

PLOYO

CRASEO

TOGHAC

I'll take some chips and a soda. Thanks!

Great! I'll be set up across the park tomorrow.

HOT DOGS $3
CHIPS $1
SODAS $2

THE MOBILE HOT DOG VENDOR
DID A GREAT BUSINESS SELLING
EVERYTHING ---

Now arrange the circled letters
to form the surprise answer, as
suggested by the above cartoon.

Print answer here ◯ ◯◯ " ◯◯◯◯ "

JUMBLE®

Unscramble these four Jumbles, one letter to each square, to form four ordinary words.

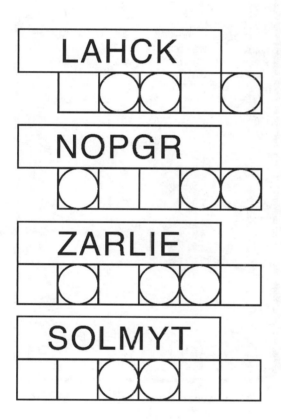

LAHCK

NOPGR

ZARLIE

SOLMYT

Looking good!

I wonder what they'll end up calling it.

THE ARCHITECT WHO DESIGNED THE PENTAGON WAS EXCITED TO SEE THE STRUCTURE ---

Now arrange the circled letters to form the surprise answer, as suggested by the above cartoon.

Print answer here

JUMBLE®

Unscramble these four Jumbles, one letter
to each square, to form four ordinary words.

CHAMT

PLUTI

MUHSUM

CLISEK

I cannot believe your
grandmother is 101!

She's
amazing!

We would go
dancing at the
Uptown Theater
every weekend.
In those days,
all the big bands
played there.

That
was in
1938?

RECALLING STORIES FROM
HER YOUTH WAS ONE OF THEIR
GRANDMOTHER'S FAVORITE ---

Now arrange the circled letters
to form the surprise answer, as
suggested by the above cartoon.

**Print
answer
here**

"⃝⃝⃝⃝ - ⃝⃝⃝⃝⃝"

JUMBLE®

Unscramble these four Jumbles, one letter to each square, to form four ordinary words.

YLLYS

ETKAW

MYLESL

BPHIOS

I'll make this quick, so you can get back to the line.

WHEN HENRY FORD WANTED TO TALK TO HIS WORKERS, HE'D HAVE THEM ---

Now arrange the circled letters to form the surprise answer, as suggested by the above cartoon.

Print answer here

JUMBLE®

Unscramble these four Jumbles, one letter to each square, to form four ordinary words.

MLUPC

RAHDO

ALMYIN

VYAICT

Ride into the future with me!

I'm in!

Driverless cars are the future! This is a great investment for us.

I'm in!

IT WAS EASY RAISING FUNDS FOR HIS BUSINESS BECAUSE INVESTORS WANTED TO ---

Now arrange the circled letters to form the surprise answer, as suggested by the above cartoon.

Print answer here

JUMBLE®

FARM

CHALLENGER PUZZLE

JUMBLE®

Unscramble these six Jumbles, one letter to each square, to form six ordinary words.

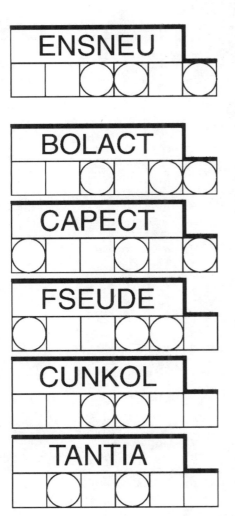

ENSNEU

BOLACT

CAPECT

FSEUDE

CUNKOL

TANTIA

I can't believe that this great apartment is available.

It has the best view in the building. It's yours if you want it.

THE ONE REMAINING APARTMENT IN THE BUILDING WAS ---

Now arrange the circled letters to form the surprise answer, as suggested by the above cartoon.

Print answer here

JUMBLE®

Unscramble these six Jumbles, one letter to each square, to form six ordinary words.

LAPRIS

RAFTEL

EGGGIL

FLONDU

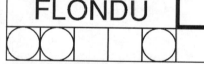

NIRWYE

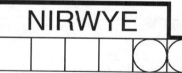

TINIFE

I guess we needed to have a reservation.

I see a lot of familiar faces.

THE TENNIS COURTS WERE FILLED WITH ---

Now arrange the circled letters to form the surprise answer, as suggested by the above cartoon.

Print answer here

JUMBLE®

Unscramble these six Jumbles, one letter to each square, to form six ordinary words.

HHENPY

GEINNS

DULCOY

BEGLIR

RWHAMT

DARMED

Look! Here are lots of rooms at the beach.

I found a resort that includes lift tickets. It's only two hours from the beach.

HE WANTED TO GO TO THE MOUNTAINS. SHE WANTED TO GO TO THE BEACH. SO THEY ---

Now arrange the circled letters to form the surprise answer, as suggested by the above cartoon.

Print answer here

JUMBLE®

Unscramble these six Jumbles, one letter
to each square, to form six ordinary words.

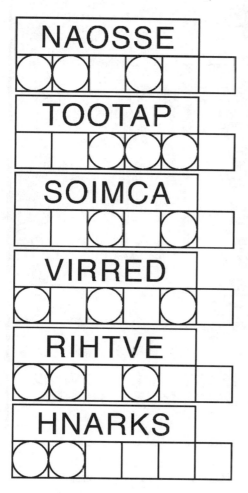

NAOSSE

TOOTAP

SOIMCA

VIRRED

RIHTVE

HNARKS

Looks like things are finally coming together.

It took a while to get this property, but my vision has become reality.

EDELWEISS ESTATES
WONDERFUL VIEWS AVAILABLE

BUILDING HOMES ON THE
MOUNTAIN WAS DIFFICULT,
BUT THE DEVELOPER ---

Now arrange the circled letters
to form the surprise answer, as
suggested by the above cartoon.

Print answer here

"⬚⬚⬚⬚⬚" ⬚⬚⬚ ON ⬚⬚

JUMBLE®

Unscramble these six Jumbles, one letter to each square, to form six ordinary words.

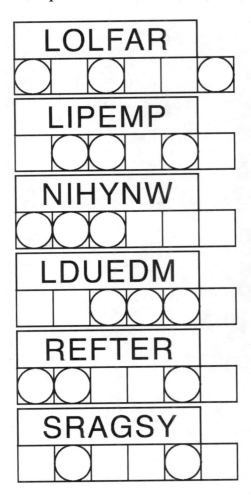

LOLFAR

LIPEMP

NIHYNW

LDUEDM

REFTER

SRAGSY

You know, you make enough money that you can hire people to maintain those.

I know! But I'm successful because I do it all.

THE OIL DRILLER WHO DIDN'T HAVE A SINGLE EMPLOYEE ---

Now arrange the circled letters to form the surprise answer, as suggested by the above cartoon.

Print answer here

JUMBLE®

Unscramble these six Jumbles, one letter to each square, to form six ordinary words.

FULFYF

NOYRRE

HIPTGL

SASNEO

TWHICS

DRREDU

I don't care how much it costs; after this winter, I need to see some color.

It's worth it.

AFTER A LONG, COLD WINTER, THE PLANT NURSERY WAS BUSY WITH PEOPLE WANTING TO ---

Now arrange the circled letters to form the surprise answer, as suggested by the above cartoon.

Print answer here

JUMBLE®

Unscramble these six Jumbles, one letter
to each square, to form six ordinary words.

RAYCEM

FUNFIP

GUMYSL

NTIBET

WRANOR

CLUTAA

Are you
sure water
can be all
three?

Why, yes!
Let me
prove it to
you.

DO LIQUIDS, SOLIDS AND
GASES HAVE MASS AND TAKE
UP SPACE? THEY DO, ---

Now arrange the circled letters
to form the surprise answer, as
suggested by the above cartoon.

Print answer here

JUMBLE®

Unscramble these six Jumbles, one letter to each square, to form six ordinary words.

CPAINT

SRUUBB

TAXFIE

LULRON

RASBBO

GTNEAL

This is a much better spread than the library convention.

Free food!

Look at how much sodium is in this.

THE LUNCH BUFFET AT THE TEXTBOOK WRITERS' CONFERENCE FEATURED A ---

Now arrange the circled letters to form the surprise answer, as suggested by the above cartoon.

Print answer here

JUMBLE®

Unscramble these six Jumbles, one letter to each square, to form six ordinary words.

LUEHPD

MARHEM

LCCAIO

NRICIO

FLEAHB

TDOYSG

It is for these reasons that I regard the decision last year to shift our efforts in space from low to high gear as among the most important decisions that will be made during my incumbency in the office of the ___ Presidency.

IN 1962, WHEN KENNEDY DECLARED WE'D LAND A PERSON ON THE LUNAR SURFACE, HE ---

Now arrange the circled letters to form the surprise answer, as suggested by the above cartoon.

Print answer here

172

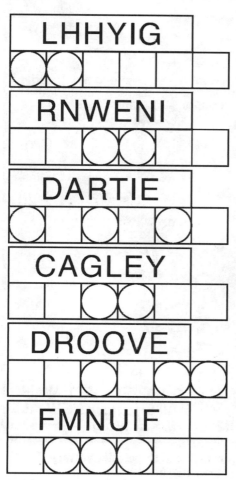

JUMBLE®

Unscramble these six Jumbles, one letter to each square, to form six ordinary words.

LHHYIG

RNWENI

DARTIE

CAGLEY

DROOVE

FMNUIF

That's all right, Sarah. These things happen. You're as honest as George Washington.

I'm so sorry. I was just swinging the poker around.

BEN FRANKLIN'S DAUGHTER DENTED THE STOVE, BUT IT DIDN'T BOTHER THE ---

Now arrange the circled letters to form the surprise answer, as suggested by the above cartoon.

Print answer here

" ⬡⬡⬡⬡⬡⬡ - ⬡⬡⬡⬡⬡ " ⬡⬡⬡⬡⬡⬡

JUMBLE®

Unscramble these six Jumbles, one letter
to each square, to form six ordinary words.

BBOASR

ADMIRI

ILOOER

CASMIO

APINDU

RUNTPI

Whoa!
All I have
are cups.

It's the Mega-
Castle Maker. I can
build a castle with
a moat in five
minutes.

HER NEW SAND BUCKET WAS
CUSTOM-MADE. SHE KNEW ALL
THE OTHERS WOULD ---

Now arrange the circled letters
to form the surprise answer, as
suggested by the above cartoon.

Print answer here

" ⬡⬡⬡⬡ " ⬡⬡ ⬡⬡⬡⬡⬡⬡⬡⬡⬡⬡⬡

JUMBLE®

Unscramble these six Jumbles, one letter to each square, to form six ordinary words.

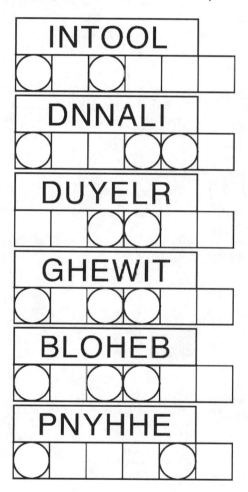

INTOOL

DNNALI

DUYELR

GHEWIT

BLOHEB

PNYHHE

What do we do? When one starts crying the next one does too.

HAPPY HAPPY JOY JOY DAY CARE

I don't know what to do with them either.

WITH THE NUMBER OF CRYING BABIES AT THE DAYCARE FACILITY, THE WORKERS WERE ---

Now arrange the circled letters to form the surprise answer, as suggested by the above cartoon.

Print answer here

○○○○○○ THE ○○○○○ - " ○○○○ "

175

JUMBLE®

Unscramble these six Jumbles, one letter to each square, to form six ordinary words.

DIOIGN

GHUTTA

RUNEMA

CTIELI

TOAANS

GLIEMN

I just love our tradition of visiting Big Ben.

Let's get the same shot as last year.

THEY'D SEEN LONDON'S FAMOUS CLOCK TOWER ON NUMEROUS OCCASIONS AND ENJOYED IT ---

Now arrange the circled letters to form the surprise answer, as suggested by the above cartoon.

Print answer here

JUMBLE®

Unscramble these six Jumbles, one letter to each square, to form six ordinary words.

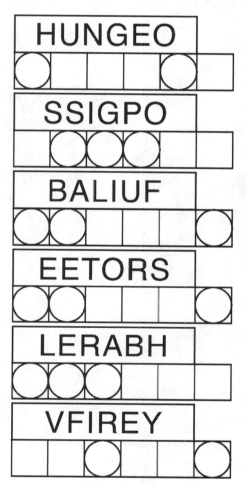

HUNGEO

SSIGPO

BALIUF

EETORS

LERABH

VFIREY

I thought he'd never leave the nest.

Look at him climb!

WHEN THE YOUNG EAGLE LEARNED TO FLY, IT WAS A ---

Now arrange the circled letters to form the surprise answer, as suggested by the above cartoon.

Print answer here

177

JUMBLE®

Unscramble these six Jumbles, one letter to each square, to form six ordinary words.

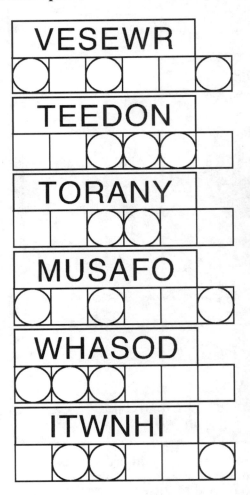

VESEWR

TEEDON

TORANY

MUSAFO

WHASOD

ITWNHI

It's a commentary on coral bleaching. With ocean temperatures rising, the coral reefs are dying.

What inspired your pattern?

SAK

WHEN THE DESIGNER TALKED TO REPORTERS ABOUT HER NEW CLOTHING LINE, SHE MADE ----

Now arrange the circled letters to form the surprise answer, as suggested by the above cartoon.

Print answer here

JUMBLE®

Unscramble these six Jumbles, one letter to each square, to form six ordinary words.

PORUTO

TOTRAH

NLUTEN

KIYLLE

NLYAMH

NGOING

THE COMEDY CLUB HAD CLOSED ABRUPTLY, WHICH WAS ---

Now arrange the circled letters to form the surprise answer, as suggested by the above cartoon.

Print answer here

179

JUMBLE®

Unscramble these six Jumbles, one letter to each square, to form six ordinary words.

DBYEOM

TUIPYP

NDAVIE

NCCILI

GNHYUR

RYUHOL

I'm glad we're finally able to get these experiments going.

It only took being 254 miles above the Earth to get to work.

THE BUSY SCIENTISTS ABOARD THE INTERNATIONAL SPACE STATION WERE ---

Now arrange the circled letters to form the surprise answer, as suggested by the above cartoon.

Print answer here

JUMBLE®

Unscramble these six Jumbles, one letter
to each square, to form six ordinary words.

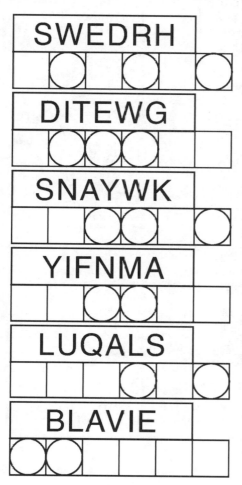

SWEDRH

DITEWG

SNAYWK

YIFNMA

LUQALS

BLAVIE

HOME
RUN!

This is so
much fun!

Whoa!
You
called
it again!

Not for the
other team.

I knew
he'd hit
another!

FIDRYCH
20

WITH THE HOME TEAM
UP 10-0, FANS IN THE
BASEBALL STADIUM WERE ---

Now arrange the circled letters
to form the surprise answer, as
suggested by the above cartoon.

Print answer here

JUMBLE®

Unscramble these six Jumbles, one letter to each square, to form six ordinary words.

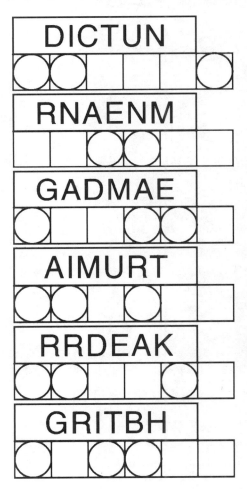

DICTUN

RNAENM

GADMAE

AIMURT

RRDEAK

GRITBH

The dealer has a six showing. The odds say you should double down on 11.

I really appreciate the help.

Your friend knows what he's talking about.

HE LEARNED HOW TO PLAY BLACKJACK THANKS TO A FRIEND WHO WAS THERE ---

Now arrange the circled letters to form the surprise answer, as suggested by the above cartoon.

Print answer here

◯◯◯◯◯◯ ◯◯◯ "◻-◯◯◯◯◯◯◯"

JUMBLE

Unscramble these six Jumbles, one letter to each square, to form six ordinary words.

GAUTOE

DASLNA

WRTMAH

GRUYSA

GAFOER

FCINET

So, I push the button and walk in a line?

Yep. Let go every 10 feet. That's about it.

THE INSTRUCTIONS FOR PAINTING THE LINES ON THE ROAD WERE ---

Now arrange the circled letters to form the surprise answer, as suggested by the above cartoon.

Print answer here

◯◯◯◯◯◯◯◯◯◯ - ◯◯◯◯◯◯◯◯◯

Answers

1. **Jumbles:** ICIER STRUM FERRET JOSTLE
Answer: She knew she wanted to be a chef after her—FIRST COURSE

2. **Jumbles:** ABOVE HURRY SNAZZY FATHER
Answer: Driving people from place to place allowed him to bring home his—"FARE" SHARE

3. **Jumbles:** INEPT WITTY MELLOW LATELY
Answer: Who is going to be the magazine's next "Person of the Year"?—TIME WILL TELL

4. **Jumbles:** GUAVA HUMOR BAKERY DRAGON
Answer: The tugboat operator was not very forgiving and known to—HARBOR A GRUDGE

5. **Jumbles:** HALVE ORBIT BUSILY TRENCH
Answer: With "Star Trek," Gene Roddenberry showed us a possible future. He was a—"TELEVISIONARY"

6. **Jumbles:** RALLY SWORN CANVAS ACTIVE
Answer: The rain had stopped. They could go to the beach now that the—COAST WAS CLEAR

7. **Jumbles:** INEPT VIPER FUNGUS IMPEDE
Answer: To see proof that the car wasn't well-cared-for, he looked at the—"EVI-DENTS"

8. **Jumbles:** FUNKY MAMBO PARDON SUNKEN
Answer: The baboons rode the carousel at the amusement park because they wanted to—MONKEY AROUND

9. **Jumbles:** LARVA GRUNT BANTER SMOOCH
Answer: The crow who considered herself to be in charge of roosting was the—BRANCH MANAGER

10. **Jumbles:** HAVOC MERGE TETHER SALMON
Answer: When "The Fantastic Four" debuted, readers bought the comic books to—MARVEL AT THEM

11. **Jumbles:** DRINK RODEO JOVIAL MEDIUM
Answer: She was becoming angrier, but, after thinking about it, it was—MIND OVER "MADDER"

12. **Jumbles:** GRILL LASSO MILDEW BEACON
Answer: He scaled Yosemite's "El Capitan" without a rope, which had onlookers—CLIMBING THE WALLS

13. **Jumbles:** AVOID WEDGE PICKUP ELEVEN
Answer: The installation of the new sink was very noisy. She wanted the plumbers to—PIPE DOWN

14. **Jumbles:** ADAGE CHAOS PROPER BABBLE
Answer: If wild pigs could live anywhere in the world, they might choose— "BOAR-A BOAR-A"

15. **Jumbles:** WEAVE PRINT DRENCH COUGAR
Answer: They used the subway to go to work every day except when it was—UNDER REPAIR

16. **Jumbles:** CREPT BLOOM SUBMIT RUFFLE
Answer: When the ram asked his adversary if he wanted to fight, he replied—"BUTT" OF COURSE

17. **Jumbles:** WAFER SUNNY DRAFTY STUDIO
Answer: Trying to identify and deal with all the different types of flu was a—STRAIN ON THE STAFF

18. **Jumbles:** IMPEL PROUD FOURTH PRICEY
Answer: The rabbits had been married for years and were a—"HOPPY" COUPLE

19. **Jumbles:** ADMIT POWER STICKY BRIGHT
Answer: The movie scene being filmed in the machine shop featured—BIT PARTS

20. **Jumbles:** LIMIT CAULK LIMBER ENTITY
Answer: The lawyer picked up new business because her happy customers were—"CLIENT-TELL"

21. **Jumbles:** LILAC MONEY SIDING CONVEX
Answer: Mary Shelley's success as an author was a result of her having—NOVEL IDEAS

22. **Jumbles:** WAIVE ADAPT MONKEY TRENDY
Answer: The fashion model was very flexible and willing to work—ANY-"WEAR" ANY TIME

23. **Jumbles:** NUTTY GOING LICHEN FASTEN
Answer: The angler knew he'd found the perfect fishing spot the moment he—CAUGHT "SITE" OF IT

24. **Jumbles:** HOTLY APART DROWSY WISELY
Answer: His claim that he could eat a hot dog in just two bites was—HARD TO SWALLOW

25. **Jumbles:** QUALM JOKER ZODIAC ZIPPER
Answer: When people first saw Count Basie perform, they were—JAZZED UP

26. **Jumbles:** TIGER CRANK HAPPEN HOMILY
Answer: His wife found out that her new ring was a cheap imitation, and now he'd—PAY THE PRICE

27. **Jumbles:** BRAVE PORCH RARELY MIRROR
Answer: It was hard to choose which new socks to buy because they were so—"COM-PAIR-ABLE"

28. **Jumbles:** FLUSH HONEY TIRADE SAFELY
Answer: The bookcase wasn't made very well and had a—SHORT SHELF LIFE

29. **Jumbles:** KNACK DITCH COUPLE GOBLET
Answer: The cat gave birth to a huge litter, and she loved the whole—"KITTEN" CABOODLE

30. **Jumbles:** HOBBY TRUTH REDEEM MUTATE
Answer: He started winning more poker tournaments after becoming a—BETTER BETTOR

31. **Jumbles:** CLOUT DADDY EFFECT CHEESE
Answer: Her father handed the business over to her, and she—SUCCEEDED

32. **Jumbles:** PRIME ENJOY KNOTTY DAINTY
Answer: He loved Kirk, Spock, the Enterprise, etc. and had a—ONE "TREK" MIND

33. **Jumbles:** BURLY DAISY CLOTHE BUBBLY
Answer: After finding contaminants in the new space capsule, the test flight had to be—SCRUBBED

34. **Jumbles:** KIOSK FORTY WEASEL UPROAR
Answer: When it comes to lighting the fuses for all the 4th of July pyrotechnic displays,—FIRE WORKS

35. **Jumbles:** HEFTY SEEDY GLITCH COLLAR
Answer: When the little girl learned to use scissors, the result was—"SHEAR" DELIGHT

36. **Jumbles:** ROUGH LOGIC WINDOW FITTED
Answer: The new plumber was very easy to get along with and happy to—GO WITH THE FLOW

37. **Jumbles:** TWIRL MESSY OPPOSE NINETY
Answer: The birthday boy swung the bat and caught the piñata right in the—SWEET SPOT

38. **Jumbles:** GUMBO HEDGE SKINNY REMOVE
Answer: They bought a home where horses were allowed and loved their—"NEIGH-BORS"

39. **Jumbles:** MUSTY SHOVE WOBBLE RODENT
Answer: When Congress created the U.S. Mint in 1792, they got their—MONEY'S WORTH

40. **Jumbles:** GROUT PRINT DOCKET OUTFIT
Answer: The Major League Soccer scout's effect on the team was—"PRO-FOUND"

41. **Jumbles:** HONOR UNITY ADMIRE ACCRUE
Answer: It was his turn at the pool table now that the previous player had—CUED HIM IN

42. **Jumbles:** PRANK VAGUE WISDOM HANDLE
Answer: The submarine in the sea between Australia and New Zealand was—DOWN UNDER

43. **Jumbles:** BOSSY BEGAN STRICT UPKEEP
Answer: When the chiropractor returned from vacation, it was—BACK TO BUSINESS

44. **Jumbles:** DIGIT HUMAN EXPAND MIDDLE
Answer: All the new dress orders had the seamstress feeling—HEMMED IN

45. **Jumbles:** HOVER SHINY MISHAP BODILY
Answer: The respectful troops called the general—
BY HIS "SIR" NAME

46. **Jumbles:** MURKY ALOHA SWEATY BURGER
Answer: The obstetricians started their business together, and now they're part of the—LABOR MARKET

47. **Jumbles:** UPPED OUTDO WISEST CRAYON
Answer: Alexander Fleming discovered antibiotics in 1928 thanks in part to him being—"CURE-IOUS"

48. **Jumbles:** HEDGE DAILY QUEASY EMBARK
Answer: Dracula's wife caught him cheating on her, and now she was going to—BLEED HIM DRY

49. **Jumbles:** BULKY SNIFF HARDER PADDLE
Answer: The washed-up coffee grower was a—HAS "BEAN"

50. **Jumbles:** LEAVE HONOR METRIC SMOGGY
Answer: When the brothers took turns wearing their grandfather's watch, it was a—TIME SHARE

51. **Jumbles:** SWEPT KAZOO DOLLAR WIRING
Answer: After the Western Hemisphere was mapped in the early 1500s, it was the—"KNEW" WORLD

52. **Jumbles:** COVET SALAD UTOPIA FALTER
Answer: The 104 satellites launched by India on a single rocket would get—SPACED OUT

53. **Jumbles:** FACET LINER DOODLE WEDDED
Answer: The computer programmer loved his new pillow because it was—DOWN-LOADED

54. **Jumbles:** BLIMP HITCH CODDLE WINERY
Answer: They hired an expert oil driller who—
DID WELL BY THEM

55. **Jumbles:** BENCH MILKY KARATE WALNUT
Answer: The cardiologist had performed the procedure so many times, she—KNEW IT BY HEART

56. **Jumbles:** ARRAY LOUSY VIOLET INFANT
Answer: When Copernicus theorized that the Earth went around the Sun, it was—REVOLUTIONARY

57. **Jumbles:** AORTA GLAND PRETTY INDOOR
Answer: King Kong's success in theaters was due to its main character,—IN LARGE PART

58. **Jumbles:** ITCHY SINGE HIATUS SPONGY
Answer: When their fusion experiment failed, the researchers were—"SIGH-ENTISTS"

59. **Jumbles:** EAGLE MOVIE SPOKEN ITALIC
Answer: The narcissists who got along so well were at the—SAME "I" LEVEL

60. **Jumbles:** SPICY WOUND CLERGY BISHOP
Answer: The golfers wanted to use the driving range, so they decided to—SWING BY THE COURSE

61. **Jumbles:** FLIRT DOUSE EFFORT STANZA
Answer: After his third bull's-eye in a row, it was clear that Vincent Van Gogh was a—"DART-IST"

62. **Jumbles:** YEAST PLANK GUITAR CEMENT
Answer: She loved all of Jagger's music, so she made a—"MICK'S" TAPE

63. **Jumbles:** ELUDE BUNCH COSMOS ZEALOT
Answer: When something starts to smell moldy and stale, it—MUST BE CLEANED

64. **Jumbles:** FOCAL CHIRP FONDUE SHRILL
Answer: They got hungry while waxing their car, so they stopped to—POLISH OFF LUNCH

65. **Jumbles:** FABLE THIEF ATTAIN PODIUM
Answer: People at the Labor Day cookout struggled when the mosquitoes—HAD A BITE TO EAT

66. **Jumbles:** PLUSH CROWD FAULTY INCOME
Answer: Once one office worker started wearing business attire to work, others—FOLLOWED SUIT

67. **Jumbles:** GIVEN NOTCH INFORM GAGGLE
Answer: Noah Webster hadn't started work on his dictionary yet, but he was—MEANING TO

68. **Jumbles:** VALET MUNCH GRAVEL OBLONG
Answer: She was transferring to their London office, so they wanted her to—GET A MOVE ON

69. **Jumbles:** NOVEL WHILE EXTORT ACIDIC
Answer: The branch didn't work for building their nest, but the birds weren't going to—DWELL ON IT

70. **Jumbles:** FUNNY GRIPE FICKLE ACCESS
Answer: No one could swim across the Paris river underwater, that would be—"IN-SEINE"

71. **Jumbles:** GOUGE DRANK HECTIC SQUISH
Answer: She wanted to start her own bread company and planned to—RAISE THE DOUGH

72. **Jumbles:** MAKER TABOO OUTING SQUARE
Answer: When it came to destroying the morning newspaper, their dog was—ON A TEAR

73. **Jumbles:** GULLY PANDA FUMBLE PAPAYA
Answer: When faced with danger, the mother bird was—UNFLAPPABLE

74. **Jumbles:** BLURT LOWLY LOADED SPLINT
Answer: After a successful evening at her weekly poker game, she enjoyed her—"WON"-DOLLAR BILLS

75. **Jumbles:** WOVEN FRESH PARADE SOLELY
Answer: The deer had a baby, and they just loved to—FAWN OVER HER

76. **Jumbles:** STALL STYLE NORMAL THRONG
Answer: When they saw the commercial for the new hearing aids, his wife was—ALL EARS

77. **Jumbles:** DERBY FIZZY FINALE BUTTON
Answer: The Mercedes driver wound through the Alps, easily negotiating the—"BENZ" IN THE ROAD

78. **Jumbles:** GROOM GRANT ELEVEN CHERRY
Answer: The farmer talked to the hens and liked to—EGG THEM ON

79. **Jumbles:** QUACK FLING RIDDEN EXCITE
Answer: They found an inventory of old sparkling water and decided it should be—LIQUIDATED

80. **Jumbles:** ESSAY CAULK POETIC MILDEW
Answer: When compared to his competition, the poker player—STACKED UP WELL

81. **Jumbles:** FORUM PRICE EXCESS BUTANE
Answer: The original version of her cookbook was a—"MENUSCRIPT"

82. **Jumbles:** STUNG OLDER THORAX BROKEN
Answer: She was able to fix her own skeet gun because she was a—TROUBLE-SHOOTER

83. **Jumbles:** GAVEL LEAKY BAFFLE PURSUE
Answer: The 600-yard par 5 was the longest hole on the course—BY FAR

84. **Jumbles:** PRONE GAUZE IGUANA HERMIT
Answer: A flock of geese was headed south for the winter, but when they'd arrive was—UP IN THE AIR

85. **Jumbles:** FLUID USHER DIVINE BURLAP
Answer: It was cold outside, so the firewood salesman—BUNDLED UP

86. **Jumbles:** FORGO PUDGY BURROW MUTINY
Answer: Their family farm had been built—
FROM THE GROUND UP

87. **Jumbles:** UNCLE LASSO PERMIT FLURRY
Answer: When Michelangelo was asked if he could create a marble statue, he said—"SCULPT-SURE"

88. **Jumbles:** HUTCH MANLY TICKET DOCTOR
Answer: They tried using machetes to cut their way through the jungle, but—COULDN'T HACK IT

89. **Jumbles:** PROVE TASTY GRASSY FIDDLE
Answer: Casinos on the "Strip" make so much money because lots of people go to—"LOSS" VEGAS

90. **Jumbles:** GROUP WHIRL EXPOSE NEGATE
Answer: When the dog moved his tail back and forth while walking, they commented on his—SWAGGER

91. **Jumbles:** KHAKI CHILL DURESS INFUSE
Answer: When the Jeep ran off the road, the giraffe was willing to—RISK HIS NECK

92. **Jumbles:** THIRD FLINT WARMLY SOOTHE
Answer: The man usually wore a toupee, but when he relaxed, he could—LET HIS HAIR DOWN

93. **Jumbles:** GLADE VITAL SWITCH IMPAIR
Answer: The new washing machine had just arrived and they were ready to—GIVE IT A WHIRL

94. **Jumbles:** GUILT PLAZA CHOPPY TROPIC
Answer: If lawmakers worked together, they could celebrate with a—POLITICAL PARTY

95. **Jumbles:** HELLO BLUFF MEADOW HARBOR
Answer: When "The Godfather" premiered in 1972, theaters were—MOBBED

96. **Jumbles:** AGENT SOUPY WRITER ENGAGE
Answer: The window company was struggling and experiencing—GROWING "PANES"

97. **Jumbles:** SWIFT RURAL EIGHTY ENGULF
Answer: When it comes to lighting a candle, using matches is usually a—SURE-FIRE WAY

98. **Jumbles:** WHOSE COUPE GUTTER TUXEDO
Answer: She was having twins and was experiencing all the things she—EXPECTED "TWO"

99. **Jumbles:** CAGEY SLANT HELMET DRIVEL
Answer: Lodging is important to the economy of the "Pine Tree State" and is considered a—"MAINE-STAY"

100. **Jumbles:** FLOOD FRONT INFAMY DELUXE
Answer: When he fell asleep on the inner tube, he—DRIFTED OFF

101. **Jumbles:** INPUT PHOTO WIGGLY BRANCH
Answer: After the plumber made all the connections to the boiler, the radiators were—PIPING HOT

102. **Jumbles:** QUEST FRAUD AFRAID BUNGEE
Answer: The price she paid for an NYC cab ride to 45th and Broadway was—"FARE" AND SQUARE

103. **Jumbles:** IGLOO NINTH SOFTEN PEWTER
Answer: Before deciding on which new scale to purchase, she wanted to—WEIGH HER OPTIONS

104. **Jumbles:** SNARL UDDER MARKET CHUBBY
Answer: He didn't look in his rearview mirror before backing up and as a result was—DUMBSTRUCK

105. **Jumbles:** DIVOT HANDY MANTRA SENTRY
Answer: When the new abacus came out, customers were ready to—HAVE "ADD" IT

106. **Jumbles:** CHOMP TOOTH JIGGLE BEANIE
Answer: James was very busy as a personal trainer with so many people—GOING TO THE "JIM"

107. **Jumbles:** EXERT FORCE CAMPUS INVOKE
Answer: For Dennis, finding room for dessert was a—PIECE OF CAKE

108. **Jumbles:** FILLY TWINE FORGOT TEACUP
Answer: The experience of using his first battery-operated toothbrush was—ELECTRIFYING

109. **Jumbles:** GOOSE SHOVE LOUNGE THRIVE
Answer: Edison filled his attic with helium because he wanted a—LIGHT HOUSE

110. **Jumbles:** FRONT THIRD OBJECT FASTEN
Answer: When Nate had to stay after school, he was—"BOARD" STIFF

111. **Jumbles:** CROSS PINCH SUNKEN POETRY
Answer: After selling almost all of his pickups, the horse was a—ONE "TRUCK" PONY

112. **Jumbles:** PIANO TRILL ACCENT ATONAL
Answer: "Loretta's voice has an arresting quality. It makes you want to…"—CALL THE POLICE

113. **Jumbles:** MIMIC POUCH LONELY DRIVER
Answer: The teen arm wrestled his dad's brother until the teen—CRIED UNCLE!

114. **Jumbles:** FAITH DEPTH EXCUSE FONDLY
Answer: You could tell that the lobsters were in love by their—DEEP AFFECTION

115. **Jumbles:** REBEL VINYL STUDIO LAGOON
Answer: Having a baby can be a lot of work because it's—LABOR INTENSIVE

116. **Jumbles:** OBESE VILLA COWARD SPIRIT
Answer: He'd failed to figure out the solution but wasn't giving up because of his—RESOLVE

117. **Jumbles:** HONEY LINER SCULPT JACKET
Answer: Acorns turn into oak trees. That's the explanation—IN A NUTSHELL

118. **Jumbles:** RANCH THYME SIMMER BENIGN
Answer: When they put a cocktail lounge on the 96th floor of the Hancock, they—SET THE BAR HIGH

119. **Jumbles:** RAINY VERGE DRESSY TIPTOE
Answer: The kids awoke to find gifts under the tree and loved the way they were—PRESENTED

120. **Jumbles:** IMPEL PRAWN VERBAL DENOTE
Answer: The horse that won lots of money for his owners was a thorough—"BRED" WINNER

121. **Jumbles:** QUOTA ENACT SCROLL FLABBY
Answer: They saw the polluted air by the smoking section and decided to—STAY CLEAR

122. **Jumbles:** TUNER TINGE GLOBAL DISOWN
Answer: When asked when he'd be done writing his new short story, the author said—IT WON'T BE LONG

123. **Jumbles:** STOMP BRINE STORMY GLANCE
Answer: The mimes had worked together for years and enjoyed being—SILENT PARTNERS

124. **Jumbles:** GRAVY WIPER PREFIX BANNER
Answer: When he proposed to her on December 31, they were able to—RING IN THE NEW YEAR

125. **Jumbles:** GOOEY SINGE THROAT FRIZZY
Answer: There was no guarantee he could become an NBA player, but he was—SHOOTING FOR IT

126. **Jumbles:** SORRY HEAVY ZODIAC TIRADE
Answer: He refused to wear his seat belt when behind the wheel, and that—DROVE HER CRAZY

127. **Jumbles:** WORRY HONEY PIGLET GRATIS
Answer: The Hoover Dam hydroelectric facility, built in the '30s, has proven its—STAYING POWER

128. **Jumbles:** SWOON VENUE ASTRAY AROUND
Answer: The billboards were so profitable, they decided to—"AD" A NEW ONE

129. **Jumbles:** KNOWN WORLD ABACUS PICKET
Answer: With the dogs getting along so well together, going for a stroll was a—WALK IN THE PARK

130. **Jumbles:** BURLY EXACT WOODEN CACKLE
Answer: If you thought Earth's center could reach 10,000 degrees Fahrenheit, you'd—BE "CORE-ECT"

131. **Jumbles:** RUNNY HEDGE ODDITY SLEEPY
Answer: The hotel room was expensive and they had no choice but to—SPEND THE NIGHT

132. **Jumbles:** RUMOR TUMMY CHOOSY BATTEN
Answer: The guy who wouldn't stop talking about how fast his boat could go was a—MOTOR MOUTH

133. **Jumbles:** AMAZE AFTER HYPHEN CONCUR
Answer: Running a marathon was invented by the—HUMAN RACE

134. **Jumbles:** FOGGY NANNY SLOWLY PETITE
Answer: The Brooklyn Bridge is one of the oldest of its kind, thanks to its—LONG LIFE SPAN

135. **Jumbles:** DROOP BUDDY ACCUSE SCRIPT
Answer: The deck used by the poker players was old. They all agreed it should be—DISCARDED

136. **Jumbles:** DRIFT KNIFE EUREKA HOLLOW
Answer: When the sisters started a business together, much of what they did was—WORK-RELATED

137. **Jumbles:** DITTO GIZMO OFFEND LESSON
Answer: She finally reached the par 5 in two shots after she—LONGED TO DO IT

138. **Jumbles:** GUEST SENSE HIPPIE FIGURE
Answer: In order to attract customers, the astrologer—PUT UP SIGNS

139. **Jumbles:** HOLLY BOUND TUSSLE HOAGIE
Answer: The store was closing, and loyal customers came in on the final day for the—LAST GOOD-"BUYS"

140. **Jumbles:** AROMA SCARF DECEIT HUMANE
Answer: For Ringo, replacing Pete Best as the Beatles' drummer—MADE HIM A "STARR"

141. **Jumbles:** TOXIN EAGLE METHOD TRUSTY
Answer: When the politician was arrested for corruption, his supporters—RAN OUT OF "ESTEEM"

142. **Jumbles:** BRAND MOGUL NOGGIN TURNIP
Answer: On the morning of the marathon, she needed to be—RUNNING ALONG

143. **Jumbles:** HYENA WAIVE BITTER GERBIL
Answer: The courtroom was brand-new, and the judge was ready to—GIVE IT A TRY

144. **Jumbles:** FLOOR SHAKY UNTOLD MISFIT
Answer: After seeing how well his hair transplant turned out, his wife said—HATS OFF TO YOU

145. **Jumbles:** TEMPO KNOWN WOBBLE TEDIUM
Answer: The table made out of mahogany was perfect, just like he—KNEW IT "WOOD" BE

146. **Jumbles:** FLEET TOPAZ EXPAND MILDER
Answer: It required fixing, so they helped repair the town clock in its—TIME OF NEED

147. **Jumbles:** PRONE CHILD MINGLE FLORAL
Answer: He wrote a letter to his old fishing buddy because he wanted to—DROP HIM A LINE

148. **Jumbles:** ONION MINCE TEMPER GROWTH
Answer: For Elizabeth, becoming Queen of England in 1952 was a—CROWNING MOMENT

149. **Jumbles:** SINGE DAISY WITHIN FLAVOR
Answer: The carpenter was stuck in traffic instead of—DRIVING NAILS

150. **Jumbles:** GAUZE RATIO MOMENT MOSAIC
Answer: When they dined in the clubhouse after a round of golf, they enjoyed the—MAIN COURSE

151. **Jumbles:** HUMID AXIOM STOOGE PLAGUE
Answer: When she saw her former husband in the restaurant, she wasn't—"EX-SIGHTED"

152. **Jumbles:** PLUME WOUND TOWARD FUTILE
Answer: He didn't initially love the idea of buying the wood stove, but he—WARMED UP TO IT

153. **Jumbles:** JUMBO DOUSE PRETTY PENCIL
Answer: The guy who wasn't tech-savvy got so frustrated with his computer that he—BOOTED IT UP

154. **Jumbles:** CHAMP TREND ORIOLE INSIST
Answer: The duration between the first and second take would depend on the—"RE-ACTION" TIME

155. **Jumbles:** TEMPT LOFTY POISON LAWYER
Answer: After a long day of shopping, the roommates came home—TOTALLY SPENT

156. **Jumbles:** ABATE LOOPY COARSE GOTCHA
Answer: The mobile hot dog vendor did a great business selling everything—A LA "CART"

157. **Jumbles:** CHALK PRONG LAZIER MOSTLY
Answer: The architect who designed the Pentagon was excited to see the structure—TAKING SHAPE

158. **Jumbles:** MATCH TULIP HUMMUS SICKLE
Answer: Recalling stories from her youth was one of their grandmother's favorite—"PAST-TIMES"

159. **Jumbles:** SLYLY TWEAK SMELLY BISHOP
Answer: When Henry Ford wanted to talk to his workers, he'd have them—ASSEMBLE

160. **Jumbles:** CLUMP HOARD MAINLY CAVITY
Answer: It was easy raising funds for his business because investors wanted to—ACCOMPANY HIM

161. **Jumbles:** UNSEEN ACCEPT UNLOCK COBALT DEFUSE ATTAIN
Answer: The one remaining apartment in the building was —LAST, BUT NOT "LEASED"

162. **Jumbles:** SPIRAL GIGGLE WINERY FALTER UNFOLD FINITE
Answer: The tennis courts were filled with—RETURNING PLAYERS

163. **Jumbles:** HYPHEN CLOUDY WARMTH ENSIGN GERBIL MADDER
Answer: He wanted to go to the mountains. She wanted to go to the beach. So they—SEARCHED HIGH AND LOW

164. **Jumbles:** SEASON MOSAIC THRIVE POTATO DRIVER SHRANK
Answer: Building homes on the mountain was difficult, but the developer—HAD HIS "SITES" SET ON IT

165. **Jumbles:** FLORAL WHINNY FERRET PIMPLE MUDDLE GRASSY
Answer: The oil driller who didn't have a single employee—DID WELL FOR HIMSELF

166. **Jumbles:** FLUFFY PLIGHT SWITCH ORNERY SEASON RUDDER
Answer: After a long, cold winter, the plant nursery was busy with people wanting to—SPRING FOR FLOWERS

167. **Jumbles:** CREAMY SMUGLY NARROW PUFFIN BITTEN ACTUAL
Answer: Do liquids, solids and gases have mass and take up space? They do,—AS A MATTER OF FACT

168. **Jumbles:** CATNIP FIXATE ABSORB SUBURB UNROLL TANGLE
Answer: The lunch buffet at the textbook writers' conference featured a—TABLE OF CONTENTS

169. **Jumbles:** UPHELD CALICO BEHALF HAMMER IRONIC STODGY
Answer: In 1962, when Kennedy declared we'd land a person on the lunar surface, he—PROMISED THE MOON

170. **Jumbles:** HIGHLY TIRADE OVERDO WINNER LEGACY MUFFIN
Answer: Ben Franklin's daughter dented the stove, but it didn't bother the—"FOUND-DING" FATHER

171. **Jumbles:** ABSORB ORIOLE UNPAID MIDAIR MOSAIC TURNIP
Answer: Her new sand bucket was custom-made. She knew all the others would—"PAIL" IN COMPARISON

172. **Jumbles:** LOTION RUDELY HOBBLE INLAND WEIGHT HYPHEN
Answer: With the number of crying babies at the daycare facility, the workers were—BEHIND THE EIGHT-"BAWL"

173. **Jumbles:** INDIGO MANURE SONATA TAUGHT ELICIT MINGLE
Answer: They'd seen London's famous clock tower on numerous occasions and enjoyed it—TIME AND TIME AGAIN

174. **Jumbles:** ENOUGH FIBULA HERBAL GOSSIP STEREO VERIFY
Answer: When the young eagle learned to fly, it was a—SIGHT FOR "SOAR" EYES

175. **Jumbles:** SWERVE NOTARY SHADOW DENOTE FAMOUS WITHIN
Answer: When the designer talked to reporters about her new clothing line, she made—FASHION STATEMENTS

176. **Jumbles:** UPROOT TUNNEL HYMNAL THROAT LIKELY NOGGIN
Answer: The comedy club had closed abruptly, which was—NO LAUGHING MATTER

177. **Jumbles:** EMBODY INVADE HUNGRY UPPITY CLINIC HOURLY
Answer: The busy scientists aboard the International Space Station were—HIGHLY PRODUCTIVE

178. **Jumbles:** SHREWD SWANKY SQUALL WIDGET INFAMY VIABLE
Answer: With the home team up 10-0, fans in the baseball stadium were—HAVING A FIELD DAY

179. **Jumbles:** INDUCT DAMAGE DARKER MANNER ATRIUM BRIGHT
Answer: He learned how to play blackjack thanks to a friend who was there—AIDING AND "A-BETTING"

180. **Jumbles:** OUTAGE WARMTH FORAGE SANDAL SUGARY INFECT
Answer: The instructions for painting the lines on the road were—STRAIGHT-FORWARD

Need More Jumbles®?

Jumble® Books

More than 175 puzzles each!

Cowboy Jumble®
$10.95 • ISBN: 978-1-62937-355-3

Jammin' Jumble®
$9.95 • ISBN: 978-1-57243-844-6

Java Jumble®
$10.95 • ISBN: 978-1-60078-415-6

Jet Set Jumble®
$9.95 • ISBN: 978-1-60078-353-1

Jolly Jumble®
$10.95 • ISBN: 978-1-60078-214-5

Jumble® Anniversary
$10.95 • ISBN: 987-1-62937-734-6

Jumble® Ballet
$10.95 • ISBN: 978-1-62937-616-5

Jumble® Birthday
$10.95 • ISBN: 978-1-62937-652-3

Jumble® Celebration
$10.95 • ISBN: 978-1-60078-134-6

Jumble® Champion
$10.95 • ISBN: 978-1-62937-870-1

Jumble® Coronation
$10.95 • ISBN: 978-1-62937-976-0

Jumble® Cuisine
$10.95 • ISBN: 978-1-62937-735-3

Jumble® Drag Race
$9.95 • ISBN: 978-1-62937-483-3

Jumble® Ever After
$10.95 • ISBN: 978-1-62937-785-8

Jumble® Explorer
$9.95 • ISBN: 978-1-60078-854-3

Jumble® Explosion
$10.95 • ISBN: 978-1-60078-078-3

Jumble® Farm
$10.95 • ISBN: 978-1-63727-460-6

Jumble® Fever
$9.95 • ISBN: 978-1-57243-593-3

Jumble® Galaxy
$10.95 • ISBN: 978-1-60078-583-2

Jumble® Garden
$10.95 • ISBN: 978-1-62937-653-0

Jumble® Genius
$10.95 • ISBN: 978-1-57243-896-5

Jumble® Geography
$10.95 • ISBN: 978-1-62937-615-8

Jumble® Getaway
$10.95 • ISBN: 978-1-60078-547-4

Jumble® Gold
$10.95 • ISBN: 978-1-62937-354-6

Jumble® Health
$10.95 • ISBN: 978-1-63727-085-1

Jumble® Jackpot
$10.95 • ISBN: 978-1-57243-897-2

Jumble® Jailbreak
$9.95 • ISBN: 978-1-62937-002-6

Jumble® Jambalaya
$9.95 • ISBN: 978-1-60078-294-7

Jumble® Jitterbug
$10.95 • ISBN: 978-1-60078-584-9

Jumble® Journey
$10.95 • ISBN: 978-1-62937-549-6

Jumble® Jubilation
$10.95 • ISBN: 978-1-62937-784-1

Jumble® Jubilee
$10.95 • ISBN: 978-1-57243-231-4

Jumble® Juggernaut
$9.95 • ISBN: 978-1-60078-026-4

Jumble® Kingdom
$10.95 • ISBN: 978-1-62937-079-8

Jumble® Knockout
$9.95 • ISBN: 978-1-62937-078-1

Jumble® Madness
$10.95 • ISBN: 978-1-892049-24-7

Jumble® Magic
$9.95 • ISBN: 978-1-60078-795-9

Jumble® Mania
$10.95 • ISBN: 978-1-57243-697-8

Jumble® Marathon
$9.95 • ISBN: 978-1-60078-944-1

Jumble® Masterpiece
$10.95 • ISBN: 978-1-62937-916-6

Jumble® Neighbor
$10.95 • ISBN: 978-1-62937-845-9

Jumble® Parachute
$10.95 • ISBN: 978-1-62937-548-9

Jumble® Party
$10.95 • ISBN: 978-1-63727-008-0

Jumble® Safari
$9.95 • ISBN: 978-1-60078-675-4

Jumble® Sensation
$10.95 • ISBN: 978-1-60078-548-1

Jumble® Skyscraper
$10.95 • ISBN: 978-1-62937-869-5

Jumble® Symphony
$10.95 • ISBN: 978-1-62937-131-3

Jumble® Theater
$9.95 • ISBN: 978-1-62937-484-0

Jumble® Time Machine: 1972
$10.95 • ISBN: 978-1-63727-082-0

Jumble® Time Machine: 1993
$10.95 • ISBN: 978-1-63727-293-0

Jumble® Trouble
$10.95 • ISBN: 978-1-62937-917-3

Jumble® University
$10.95 • ISBN: 978-1-62937-001-9

Jumble® Unleashed
$10.95 • ISBN: 978-1-62937-844-2

Jumble® Vacation
$10.95 • ISBN: 978-1-60078-796-6

Jumble® Wedding
$9.95 • ISBN: 978-1-62937-307-2

Jumble® Workout
$10.95 • ISBN: 978-1-60078-943-4

Jump, Jive and Jumble®
$9.95 • ISBN: 978-1-60078-215-2

Lunar Jumble®
$9.95 • ISBN: 978-1-60078-853-6

Monster Jumble®
$10.95 • ISBN: 978-1-62937-213-6

Mystic Jumble®
$9.95 • ISBN: 978-1-62937-130-6

Rainy Day Jumble®
$10.95 • ISBN: 978-1-60078-352-4

Royal Jumble®
$10.95 • ISBN: 978-1-60078-738-6

Sports Jumble®
$10.95 • ISBN: 978-1-57243-113-3

Summer Fun Jumble®
$10.95 • ISBN: 978-1-57243-114-0

Touchdown Jumble®
$9.95 • ISBN: 978-1-62937-212-9

Oversize Jumble® Books

More than 500 puzzles!

Colossal Jumble®
$19.95 • ISBN: 978-1-57243-490-5

Jumbo Jumble®
$19.95 • ISBN: 978-1-57243-314-4

Jumble® Crosswords™

More than 175 puzzles!

Jumble® Crosswords™
$10.95 • ISBN: 978-1-57243-347-2